The Art of Intentional Dressing

YOUR ESSENTIAL STYLE GUIDE FOR MANIFESTING A MAGNETIC LIFE

THE ART OF INTENTIONAL DRESSING

ERIN WALSH

HARPERONE

An Imprint of HarperCollins*Publishers*

HarperCollins books may be purchased for educational, business, or sales promotional use. For information, please email the Special Markets Department at SPsales@harpercollins.com.

hc.com

FIRST EDITION

Designed by Bonni Leon-Berman

Art © Kaitlin Walsh

Library of Congress Cataloging-in-Publication Data has been applied for.

ISBN 978-0-06-348364-4

Printed in the United States of America

26 27 28 29 30 LBC 5 4 3 2 1

To my mother, Jane, and her mother, Jane,

who inspired me to be intentional and

aligned in all things—especially in style

Contents

Foreword

BY ANNE HATHAWAY

I t would seem history loves a 'fit.

Some of the best, most beloved, and widely known stories in all of humanity wouldn't be the same without clothes.

Eve reaches for forbidden fruit, and instantly invents the concept "having nothing to wear."

An emperor doesn't trust his own eye, and learns the hard way that style is not what others say it is.

Cinderella's entire socioeconomic reality is elevated by a single, well-timed look.

While it is common wisdom that you can never judge a book by its cover, and common decency to never judge someone because of the clothes they wear, it's also common courtesy to remember your place because everyone puts their pants on one leg at a time.

These stories and enduring truisms make sense to us because of the simple fact that the majority of the world has to get dressed every single day. Often the first question one asks themselves once they get out of bed is "what am I going to wear?" Despite the daily predictability of this question, so many people—including myself from time to time—can find it screamingly hard to answer. Perhaps that is because the question's underlying subtext is so loaded and dimensional. The question tugging at the thread of "what am I going to wear?" is usually "why do I care?" And the big question at the heart of it all is "who am I?"

You may be someone who genuinely doesn't care—and that's totally cool! You may think that we would all be better off if we wore the same thing, that time spent worrying about what to wear is time wasted, that fashion is only for the "silly" and "frivolous." If that's your style, enjoy!

If, however, you find yourself instinctively drawn to the idea that who you are is somehow connected to what you choose to wear—and you desire a greater depth of understanding of what that might mean for you—you have found the right book.

As for me, I think it is always important to remember that while personal circumstances absolutely dictate the availability of options, it's equally very, *very* important to recognize money can't buy style.

Style is not bought—it is created. Style is about communication—either by revealing something or by withholding something. Fashion is only ever about one thing: your personal relationship to it.

I don't mean to make light of means—having a budget that allows for expensive clothing is a privilege few enjoy, and having access to the work (and in my case, the generosity) of the best designers in the world can absolutely improve your closet. Further, having the funds that allow you to keep up with ever-evolving tastes and styles might also mean you are free from the stress that comes with the nuts-and-bolts realities of life, like paying for housing and putting food on the table; that sort of economic ease must not be discounted, as it makes all aspects of life less stressful, including getting dressed.

Whatever your financial situation, it remains true that labels aren't everything and having the latest hot accessory will not improve your happiness if you don't first understand the person holding the handbag. If you are someone who can't afford whatever this moment's "it" bag is, I hope you know you are not excluded from experiencing delight as you explore—and hopefully enjoy—your own style.

I saw this from an early age in my own family. Neither of my grandmothers could be described as wealthy, but they had *style*. Neither of them were in a position to buy top-shelf designers, but they always looked amazing and totally themselves. One was French and lovely: She favored tailored minimalism—beautiful lines with statement accessories. The other was Philadelphian and fabulous—when she passed we found a giraffe-print '70s style suit in the back of one of her closets and piles of bold costume jewelry.

They couldn't have been more different in their choices, but they were both inspiring in how specific they were in how they chose to present themselves to the world.

Erin Walsh, my slightly psychic bestie, soul sister, fellow crystal lover, and the author of the wonderful book you are about to read, has become my family. Erin reminds me a lot of my grandmothers: She is like a warm hug, a sentient beam of light. She is nurturing, caring, wonderful to have in your life, and while I'm always excited to see her because of how fun and darling she is, I'm also excited because, like with my grandmothers, I am *dying* to know how she put herself together that day.

The "grandmother energy" connection I feel with her is so present that we have a pet name for each other: GWFG (gwiffgee). It means: God Willing, Future Grandmas. We are both women figuring out how to harmonize our busy work lives with our busier personal lives with the shared goal of manifesting a future where we will find ourselves somewhere peaceful, draped in gorgeous caftans, playing with our cherished grandchildren who are *also* best friends.

And while we look forward to a future that contains light, love, and leisure, for now we don't actually have a ton of time to think about what we wear every day. As lucky as we are, we are gals who gotta work to make it happen (after all, isn't manifesting without muscle just daydreaming?). Right now, she and I are focused on building the lives we want by following the wisdom of everyone's greatest grandmother, Eve: After the fall, Eve worked with what she had, and she acquired knowledge as she lived.

Style is not one fixed thing that needs to be gotten "right": it is an ongoing dance, an art form like any other, as blessedly infinite as your imagination.

Like Cinderella, I love when a magic gown appears (who wouldn't?), but the practical reality of my life is that I need to pivot from drop-off to basketball courts to movie sets to red carpets to boardrooms to whatever surprises the day throws at me. I love all the myriad aspects of my life, and I don't want to feel stressed worrying that one of the parts of myself will somehow work against the whole. Like everyone (especially women), my life contains multitudes and I do not want to constrict any aspects of myself in fear of "getting it wrong." I don't expect to have it all, but I do want to always feel like myself, wherever I go.

With Erin's help, I have found a style that I feel has expanded to fit my life. As my stress about clothes has decreased, a certain boldness and joy has emerged. I find I am more adventurous, and that has made me connect more deeply to feeling powerful. There are so many things in the world I can't control. How I feel about the daily choice of what I wear is something I can; how lovely to be in a place where I can appreciate the enjoyment of that, and how grateful I am to Erin to have guided me there.

The gift of this book is that Erin has made clear that the only thing you need to dress well—an entirely personal definition—is an understanding of what your life needs and the self-worth to want to feel your best. She has given you the tools to literally CREATE your own experience of your day. No, this book won't stop your boss from yelling at you unfairly or make that jerk who cut you off be a less awful driver, but it will make you the boss of your own closet and make you feel you cannot be driven off the road where you are heading.

The reason you will feel that way is because you will have learned to unleash the magic that is already inside of you, just waiting for a friend. (Spoiler alert: It's you. The friend is you.)

What a gift to have a fashion insider tell you that your happiness and self-fulfillment is more powerful than any label, by spreading the message that you yourself are already more than enough.

Just as clothes are a key part of so many of our greatest stories, they are a key part of your life too.

I hope you know you deserve a great story.

Good luck, and happy adventuring! xx

Introduction

"The biggest adventure you
can ever take is to live the
life of your dreams."

OPRAH WINFREY

Most people—in particular, most *women*—open their closets each morning and pull out something that makes them feel bad about themselves. Sounds masochistic, right? I mean, why would we do this to ourselves? Well, it could be the result of a frantic morning schedule or a wardrobe of misfitting clothes or trying too hard to stay on trend or having no clue about how we really want to show up in the world or . . . lots of other things.

But since choosing what to put on is a daily exercise, in a way, hating what you end up in subjects you needlessly to self-inflicted micro-traumas day after day. Here's what I mean by that: It might not seem like a huge deal when something doesn't fit right, or you walk into a meeting or special event or even just the day's errands feeling less than amazing. But when we resign ourselves to this subpar status on a daily basis, it erodes our confidence and robs us of the joy that getting dressed has the potential to bring. And that *is* a very big deal. After all, how can we be our best selves, reach peak performance at work, and thrive in our relationships when we leave the house feeling like crap? We can't. And, we don't have to!

I know Fashion (with a big F) can be intimidating. But I'm going to use the word anyway because the fashion I'm talking about is available to everyone. My brand of fashion is the kind that can help us all express our most authentic selves because what we *wear* is an essential part of communicating who we *are*; our clothes transmit a nonverbal signal to everyone who sees us. That's one reason it's vital to spend adequate time thinking about your personal style vibe—and how it's received by others. But way more important than how the outside world assesses you is how *you* feel about *you*. I'm here to teach you how what you put on your body can transform your life. That's not an overstatement; it's a deep and passionate belief I have developed working as a stylist for nearly two decades and through serious contemplation about how fashion fits into my own life, personally.

Funny thing is, I didn't set out to be a stylist—it was a happy accident. I went to New York University to study acting and graduated with a fine arts degree in theater. But soon after graduation, I found it impossible to see the path forward. My decision to give up acting and start over in a new career—in what, I didn't yet know—was an instinctual choice. It was just this inner knowing that whispered "DO NOT PROCEED." That pivot away from acting was one of the first times I really listened to my intuition when making a significant life decision. The only way I can explain it is to say that something in me knew that life had other plans.

I have always loved clothes and playing dress-up; the idea of wearing costumes is probably part of what drew me to acting in the first place. And for as long as I can remember, even as a little girl, I have been told that I should work in fashion. I mostly brushed off that idea, thinking it would be a silly line of work. I was seeking purpose. So in my purposeless post-NYU era, I tried a few different things: I went from working in fashion retail to doing a stint in public relations to landing my first major style-related gig as an assistant in the fashion department at *Vogue*.

It was all very *The Devil Wears Prada*, which actually hit theaters the same year (2006) I landed that job. I remember stepping off the elevator on my first day, seeing the giant *Vogue* logo in front of me, and thinking, *"This is where I will be for the next thirty years." Vogue* was unparalleled in fashion media—and being there, with the best of the best, made me feel as stunned, awed, and terrified as Dorothy was when she landed in Oz. There was an unspoken pressure to be chic and fabulous. You had to find a way to be just that (or borrow it from the closet). It was "fake it 'til you make it" fashion boot camp.

It was also a place with sky-high standards of excellence in all realms—nothing was deemed too hard to pull off. As my then-boss warned me: "No doesn't exist here." If you didn't know where to source a prop for a shoot, you had to be exceedingly industrious and resourceful. Once, for a Comme des Garçons tribute shoot photographed by Irving Penn, my fashion assistant bestie, Phoebe de Croisset, and I resourced props at both a culinary school and the sex shops on Christopher Street in the West Village! What has stuck with me most about my *Vogue* experience is that there is *always* a solution. It's just a matter of getting creative enough to find it. I remind my current assistants of this if ever panic breaks out over a missing shoe!

Years later, I went on to work with Anne Hathaway, the very star of *The Devil Wears Prada* herself. She's still a cherished client of mine today and the perfect person to write this book's foreword, not to mention a soulmate friend. The much-anticipated sequel to that movie is being shot as I type these words. As paparazzi videos of the NYC street scenes from the shoot fill my social media feed, I'm brought right back to my time in the *Vogue* fashion closet, which sparks a bit of nostalgia for how remarkable the magazine world was then—filled with creative powerhouses whose big imaginations (and budgets to match) turned out print issues that were artistic keepsakes. That entire industry has changed dramatically to one that favors quickly produced digital content that feeds consumers' voracious appetites, as well as their atrophying attention spans. Gone are the days when you'd flip through the pages of a magazine and be transported to exotic locations. It still happens, just a lot less often.

What hasn't changed: Our need for fashion to inspire us, to ignite our imaginations, and to outwardly tell our innermost stories.

It's been almost twenty years since I walked into that *Vogue* office, and when I look back now, I feel a lot of compassion for the young, wide-eyed assistant I was then. It's so disheartening when we don't feel like we measure up. I got good at dressing the part of the confident fashion person, but it took about ten thousand more hours to actually *believe* I was one—to embrace the title of "fashion expert" enough to counsel people on what they should wear, let alone write a book about it. First, I had to heal my own relationship with dressing.

Maybe you've also tried to just dress the part—to get a job in a certain industry or to fit into a certain social group. It can work for the short term. You can successfully fool yourself and others. But over time, your authentic wants and needs begin to bubble up and at that point, you can either push them back down for a while or you can let them breach the surface. Using clothes as a mask or a mirage just isn't sustainable. Or enjoyable! Besides, it's not enough to dress the part. You deserve to *feel* the part.

What I want you to commit to is THE PROCESS ✓

And contrary to popular belief, fashion isn't a luxury, as my friend Jennifer Hyman, co-founder of the pioneering designer clothing rental platform Rent the Runway, reminded me. Everyone needs to get dressed every day, the same as they need to brush their teeth. But fashion has developed a rep for being aloof and unattainable—and many women view it as something of a nemesis. I plan to reverse that trend by guiding you in a way that empowers you to see how fashion can become your closest ally in living a life of your own design.

After *Vogue*, my independent career got going. I assisted several top freelance stylists and eventually broke out on my own. Steadily, I grew my business working with fantastic women such as Sarah Jessica Parker, Maggie Gyllenhaal, Kristen Wiig, and Kerry Washington. *The Hollywood Reporter* began consistently listing me as one of the top celebrity stylists. There were so many pinch-me-this-can't-be-real moments: exhilarating awards seasons, Met Galas, fashion campaigns, and international travel. I also met and married Christian, a wonderful, handsome photographer from Sweden, and soon after, I became a mother. (I now have three beautiful children.) I successfully juggled fashion and family—and for a while, I was thriving.

But over time, questions started creeping into my mind about whether my chosen career had any purpose beyond selling clothes and helping clients shine under the red-carpet spotlight. The wellspring of creativity and excitement that fashion had always roused in me seemed to be running dry. I again felt that whisper of intuition, this time telling me I needed to play a part in shifting the rampant dis-ease women have with their bodies and getting dressed.

During the Covid lockdown, with the world on an indefinite pause, I had more time than usual to look inward.

I have always dabbled in self-growth books and consider myself a spiritual person in the sense that I'm comforted by the idea that we are all part of something bigger—a collective of shared, supportive energy. During my downtime you're apt to find me curled up with a spiritual or self-help book. I'm committed to my constant inner development and to finding ways to get the most mileage out of my limited free time—especially since I'm balancing a young family on top of my career as a celebrity fashion stylist. I can pick up books such as my friend Gabrielle Bernstein's *Super Attractor* (love, love, love!) when my energetic kids aren't gathered around my legs or crawling into my lap—or when I have a quiet moment on a photo or film set. These books help me get honest about my goals and then inspire me to go after them in an unattached way.

Self-development authors such as Glennon Doyle and Brené Brown remind me life can be messy and great at the same time and that vulnerability is a superpower. My client Selena Gomez does the same. Her transparency about her own mental health struggles has no doubt helped millions feel less shame about theirs. All of these women promote a fierce form of self-truth and acceptance that appeals to me. One of my all-time favorite authors—and the first one who really ignited a spark in me—is the late Louise Hay, who founded the trailblazing publishing company Hay House. In 1984 she published *You Can Heal Your Life,* in which she explained how she believed that physical symptoms in our bodies are interwoven with our emotional experiences—that discomfort and disease are tied to unprocessed trauma, emotional triggers, and more.

While cloistered from the outside world, I reread passages from Louise Hay's book, which sparked an epiphany for me. Until then, I was operating the way I assume many fashion industry people do, focusing mostly on how clothes *look* (no shock there, I guess). I hadn't consciously considered the much deeper connection between what we wear and how we *feel*. Or that how we dress could affect us on such a visceral, whole-body level and impact our vibrational frequency.

Quick primer on what I mean when I refer to vibrational frequency, according to those more versed in the fundamentals of physics than I am: Simply put, everything in the universe is energy. Even objects that appear to be stationary are, in fact, vibrating. Think back to your high school physics lessons where you likely first heard about Einstein's famous equation ($E = mc^2$), which demonstrates that mass and energy are interchangeable; matter is simply energy in a concentrated form. This means every atom in your body represents dynamic energy in constant motion—that is, you are composed of particles that vibrate at specific frequencies.

This law of vibration becomes meaningful (and more applicable) when you understand that everything around you—as well as *within* you—is in constant motion. From the molecular vibrations that create heat, like the warmth you feel from holding a mug of tea, to the resonant frequencies powering technologies such as MRI machines and even the vibrating strings of a musical instrument that send waves through the air. This principle governs energy flow in your daily life, whether you're aware of it or not.

What's really exciting is that you can learn to be more aware of it so you can work more consciously with these vibrational states, influencing how you harmonize with certain elements, such as subtle energies you feel in social interactions. I bet you've felt subtle energies, even if you didn't have the language to explain those inklings at the time. Recall an occasion when a person entered a room you were in (a work meeting, book club, or dinner with friends) and the mood shifted. You could just feel it "in the air," whether for better or worse. That's the subtle energy I'm talking about.

I know that's a lot of science to drop in a style-focused book, but there is so much beauty and potential in these concepts. Your thoughts, actions, emotions, and *intentions* create patterns of energy that interact with the energetic field in the environment. Rather than being separate and isolated, you're an interconnected expression of energy, naturally resonating with everything around you.

In 2022, three physicists were awarded the Nobel Prize for their experiments on a phenomenon called "quantum entanglement."[1] Their work showed that deeply linked particles can remain connected in such a way that the state of one particle instantly influences the state of another, even when separated by large distances. This concept was first surfaced in the 1930s, and back then, Einstein himself was skeptical of what he called "spooky action at a distance," proving that sometimes even geniuses have a hard time believing the unbelievable.[2]

I find comfort in quantum entanglement because, to me, it validates why I feel close to my kids even when we are apart physically. Or why some people, me included, say they remain connected to loved ones who have passed away. I'm sure this isn't how the scientists would explain their findings, but their work speaks to an everlasting continuum of connectedness—and I'm warmed by that idea.

Even if you just boil it down to the basics, vibrational frequency alone holds empowerment: You are not a fixed, limited being; you are an evolving expression of energy with the potential for transformation. The main takeaway: The inherent malleability of your vibrational nature allows you to change and create the reality you envision. Read that line again.

How so? Vibrational frequency can be influenced by thoughts, emotions, physical health, the environment, spiritual practices, and more. Positive emotions such as love, joy, and gratitude are believed to *increase* vibrational frequency, while negative emotions such as fear, anger, and sadness are thought to *lower* it.

Now, whether you can measure your vibe is complicated because there is a difference between physics and metaphysics. Physics examines the observable universe, focusing on motion, forces, energy, and the structure of matter. Metaphysics explores more abstract ideas: existence, reality, identity, and whether anything exists beyond the physical world. Instead of relying on direct observation or mathematics, metaphysics utilizes philosophical reasoning, anecdotal data, and conceptual analysis.

Rather than go down this rabbit hole, I want to challenge you to not worry about qualifying your frequency and to instead tune in to becoming more aware of the energetic shifts you *feel* in yourself and in the world around you. The light-bulb moment for me was experiencing just how impactful what we wear is on how we *feel*— our emotional state, which in turn impacts not only us but everyone around us through the energy we emit.

That was a potent realization for me and precisely what I needed to imbue my work with more meaning. I wasn't just getting people glammed up for fancy events; I was helping them step into their true power—their true selves. Once I was tuned in to this idea—*that how we feel about what we wear impacts us and those around us in remarkable ways*—I wanted to share this knowledge. Correction: I *had* to share this knowledge. I've spent a lot of time mentally deconstructing the process I have been using for years when choosing clothes (and how to style them) for my clients. As soon as I started lacing intention into every aspect of my being and my life, I realized that everything was better when injected with purpose and direction: relationships, getting in better shape, pursuing work goals, everything. And as for the fashion part? Dressing is so much more meaningful and effortless when we start with the *why*.

Whether we realize it or not, there's a conversation happening between our clothing and our subconscious. In fact, some interesting research has been done around a psychological phenomenon called "enclothed cognition." It has shown that the symbolic meaning you attach to clothing actually affects how you think and act. Imagine that moment when you put on something that represents strength to you—whether it's a black blazer or a flowy dress and your mind begins to possess the qualities you've wrapped around your physical form.

When you consider this, your wardrobe morphs into a collection of potential selves waiting to be activated. The original study on enclothed cognition, conducted by psychologists Hajo Adam and Adam Galinsky in 2012, involved participants wearing identical white coats that were described either as a "doctor's coat" or a "painter's coat."[3] The researchers found that participants who believed they were wearing a "doctor's coat" performed better on attention-related cognitive tasks than those who thought they were wearing a "painter's coat." This demonstrates that the symbolic meaning attributed to clothing—what we *believe* about what we wear—can measurably influence our behavior and become part of our lived experience.

The garments you choose each morning aren't just covering your body; they're programming your inner reality by summoning aspects of yourself you wish to cultivate. This all reinforces my deepest belief and the reason I wrote this book: What you wear can have a powerful effect on your life!

Back when I began developing my method of dressing, I didn't even know I was developing anything. It was just an experimental process: trial and error, practical applications of loose ideas, monitoring real-time responses. At a certain point, my work drew a comprehensive response. I'd know for better or worse how the outfits I styled impacted the wearer (my clients), and what fans and the media thought (no lack of opinions there!).

The chapters that follow are an amalgamation of everything that contributed to the creation of my dressing method—a clear approach for curating a wardrobe and creating a personal style that serves a more important function than just sheathing your naked body. This method can move you in the direction of your desires. And though I've been using aspects of this process for years, it wasn't until I sat down to write this book that I put it into an organized format anyone can follow and benefit from.

If this sounds like it's going to be a lot of work, it's not! You're going to have to trust me here. Soon using this way of dressing will become second nature to you, too.

So what is this method of mine?

It's called CREATE, an acronym for the framework I've devised for making style choices more intentionally to elevate your self-confidence, communicate your true essence, and inspire changes that help materialize your authentic dreams. Yes, your daily dressing decisions represent an opportunity to influence your self-actualization. By habitually using the CREATE method, you will come to understand that the way clothes make you *feel* has a cascading effect on every aspect of your life.

I'll be walking you through each step in the coming chapters, while also taking fun little detours to allow other expert voices in fashion, style, spirituality, self-development, and science to provide valuable insights that amplify and expand the concepts you'll be learning about.

The truth is, enacting this method rescued me from the relentless hamster wheel of doing. And then, doing more. You can't have it all, they say. And then there are times, as a working mother or any woman walking this earth, that you can't seem to do one damn thing right!

I once sent my kids to visit their grandparents in Sweden without having packed a single pair of pajamas or underwear. I've lost count of the number of parent-teacher conferences (um, every single one of them) I've had to reschedule because my calendar is constantly changing. And just recently, I had to have my Uber make a pit stop at a boutique on the way to an event so I could buy shoes because I forgot to throw heels in my gym bag when I left the house that morning and there was no time to go home to grab them.

Whether we're in a funk or just burned out, we all feel that stirring to reboot our lives—to shed old versions of ourselves and reconnect with our deepest truth. My season of seeking kept returning me to that perennially one-word question: Why? As in, why don't I feel more content? And also, what can I do to change that?

While searching for answers, the universe conspired in my favor. When we moved from NYC to LA, I was introduced almost immediately to Valerie Mya, a healer whose specific gift lies in awakening others to their capacity for self-healing, which is a continuous journey, not a one-and-done project.

I sat on Valerie's couch and watched the hummingbirds just outside the window dart around her garden. I was nervous. I didn't have much experience with healers at the time, and I didn't even know what I wanted or why, exactly, I was there. I only knew that my intuition had been interjecting with the thought: "*It's time to step into your more.*" I was wrestling with that inner monologue when Valerie simply asked, "In one word, how do you want to *feel*?" The answer populated my brain immediately. "Serene," I answered. I wanted to feel at peace and in alignment. I wanted serenity.

My life had been feeling slightly chaotic. I had a fast-paced, detail-dependent job that required a lot of traveling, and a growing family that depended on me, and we had undertaken a move (temporarily, it turns out) to the opposite coast. And even during the pandemic, when I wasn't traveling, the survival-mode energy coupled with my insatiable desire to support my family and excel in my career was exhausting. It was *mostly* good things. I was grateful. But "positive stress" is still stress. And there are only so many hours in a day to get it all done. The inflection point for me was realizing that if I wanted to maintain the pace of my burgeoning life (I did!), I couldn't expect the peace offering to come from the outside; the serenity I was craving needed to come from within me, and then perhaps I could extend it out to the various areas of my life.

That unlock became my mantra. After the session, I started letting the word *serenity* permeate everything I did, everything I wore, everything I touched. I started moving a little more slowly and deliberately—no rushing between tasks; I spoke in a softer, more measured tone during conversations and I made it a practice to listen closely instead of just waiting to speak; I enacted little rituals like lighting a candle, palo santo, or sage to signal that the work day was over. I changed outfits throughout the day (often switching into a housedress at dinnertime to cook) to better demarcate the day so I could be more present in each part of it. I began buying and arranging flowers on a weekly basis to honor our home and make it feel more beautiful, inviting, and serene. In the car or on walks, I listened almost exclusively to self-help or inspirational podcasts and audiobooks. I researched feng shui, rearranging our furniture, photos, and home color palette for more calm, clear alignment, and I did the same at my office space. As for clothes, I avoided wearing patterns or bold colors; my preferred palette became every conceivable shade of white. These changes made all the difference for me as I stepped into the life of serenity I was seeking.

Ultimately, dressing with intention empowers you to use clothes as a catalyst for self-growth; it's an entry point into a deeper exploration of how you want to live your life.

This may all sound lofty or "woo-woo" right now, but if you stick with me you'll see. The process I use with each and every person I dress—from celebrities to those who want to embody main character energy in their own lives—has had a profound impact on their ability to magnetize the life they want.

When we dress with intention and feel good about ourselves and the direction we're moving in, those feelings emanate. In other words, feeling good begets feeling good. And it drives our life performance. Legendary Olympic runner Florence Griffith Joyner (aka Flo-Jo) knew this. The three-time gold medalist dressed in the most unconventional, eye-catching "athletic" attire in vibrant colors and cuts: custom one-legged tracksuits, some of them made of lace. She wore makeup and jewelry, styled her hair, and her statement nails were super long and ornate. She was the embodiment of strength, femininity, and power. Flo-Jo's reported motto: "Dress good to look good. Look good to feel good. And feel good to run fast." What an icon.

Another icon who truly understands the power of dressing with intention is the fashionable South Carolina–bred, LA–based interior designer Kelly Wearstler. She is a bold visionary who has made an indelible mark on interior design with her fearless use of color, luxurious textures, and that perfect mix of vintage and contemporary. She's the creative force behind stunning hotel transformations such as the Viceroy and the Proper Hotel brands— not to mention showstopping homes for A-list clients. She is not afraid to go big with creativity. And she is just as fearless when it comes to fashion.

I was floored one day while reading her addictive Substack newsletter, *WearstlerWorld*. This particular dispatch was dedicated to detailing how she chooses what to wear every day—or, shall we say, intentional dressing. For her, picking an outfit isn't just about looking good (which she always does); it's about stepping into her most authentic, creative self each day. Kelly revealed how she uses her wardrobe as a creative catalyst and, she added, as "a broadcast: a subliminal tool for when I present to clients, or when I want to send a message to the studio [staff]."[4]

Kelly posed these questions aimed at how we approach dressing each morning: "How do you treat yourself? And, what do you want to say to the world around you?" She's transformed daily dressing into a "tool for expression, even productivity, meant to capture shifts in intention, attitude, ambition. . . . It's about creating and keeping up my own momentum."

Kelly's thoughtful approach is an extraordinary example of how we can infuse intention into our own dressing rituals, turning that seemingly routine or mundane moment into an opportunity for growth, creativity, and authentic expression!

Feeling good about how you look enhances your ability to attract better opportunities into your life. Flo-Jo used it to clear hurdles and Kelly uses it to create a robust life and career. And those are just two early examples to get you amped up. Satisfaction with your appearance boosts self-esteem, which is communicated to others through your body language and the general state of your being. As you interact with people, this positivity is often reciprocated in social reactions, which further reinforces your higher self-image, creating a cycle psychologists call an "upward spiral." Your improved mindset makes you more open to opportunities, more willing to take risks, and more resilient when facing challenges. All of that naturally leads to better outcomes and experiences.

To be sure, dressing with intention with my CREATE method is a unique approach, but I know you're on board because you're here!

And I want to thank you for being here. Utilizing something as habitual as getting dressed is both a practical and a super fun way to conduct self-growth work. I'm not claiming it's the *only* work you'll ever need to do to bring your dreams to reality, but it's going to point you in the right direction in a major and meaningful way.

I want this book to be an evergreen resource that you can return to when your life circumstances change, as they inevitably will, or just when you're looking for a little extra advice and guidance. I'm on a mission to make your dressing life easier, so it was important to me to make this process feel like a pleasurable pursuit, not labor.

This book can kick-start and shepherd transformation and creation—your own fashion alchemy. The word *alchemy* was originally defined as a medieval chemical science aimed at the transmutation of base metals into gold. It has since expanded to apply to any process that changes something in a somewhat mysterious way. The fashion alchemy I want you to experiment with is intended to transform the way you think (and ultimately feel) about dressing. At times the changes it ignites may seem mysterious, but just go with it!

To bring this guide to you, I dove into research and interviewed some of my favorite thinkers in the fields of spirituality, self-development, psychology, neuroscience, style, and more. And while I personally bring my fashion acumen, CREATE method, and ever-expanding spiritual knowledge to every page, I also wanted to be the conduit to best-in-class info from every area of expertise I thought might help you. You'll hear from many people in the coming chapters; some of them were already part of my inner circle and now I count many more of these amazing contributors as friends. We're uploading a lot of information for you to download, but don't let it overwhelm you. Take it in, and use the parts that speak to you most to form your own fashion alchemy.

Since I'm both a dreamer and a doer, this book is rooted in what I call practical magic—meaning there are some aspects that require a leap of faith, but many others that yield immediate and tangible benefits. I also included simple exercises throughout the book to help you assimilate the information and to gift you with takeaways to put to work today.

One final note: The majority of my clients are women, so that's where my expertise lies and the audience I speak directly to (most of the experts I consulted are women, too). That said, the messages I convey are universal—they can work for anyone and everyone, regardless of gender identity. I also want to stress that empowering yourself through your wardrobe is not a luxury concept; it's a mindset and a modus operandi that is available to everyone.

I learned so much writing this book. I put my heart, soul, and vast experience with how style impacts our reality into every page. I know after reading it you'll feel more in control of your closet—and your destiny.

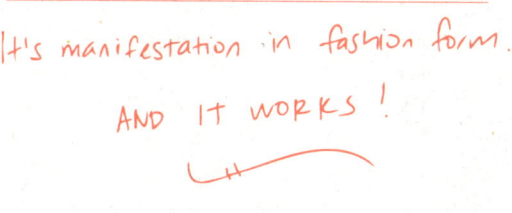

It's manifestation in fashion form.
AND IT WORKS !

Why You Don't Know What the Eff to Wear

"When you know your goal, intuition stops making you crazy and starts finding your opportunity."

LAURA DAY

Every morning, millions of women share the same struggle: choosing what the eff to wear. I'm guessing you're one of them. The scene looks something like this: You stare blankly into your closet because the seemingly simple task of getting dressed feels impossible for some reason. Before long, discarded clothes are strewn everywhere and you're stressing about how long it's taking to figure out what the eff to wear when you have so many other things you need to be doing. This is essentially how things play out for nearly every woman I've encountered in my both personal and professional life.

I see you standing there. And I want to help.

Not being able to figure out what the eff to wear has become such a vexing, universal problem for women. It's not for lack of clothes or lack of style or lack of ability to make decisions in general. It's more nuanced than that. In fact, it's not really about the clothes themselves. I know that sounds strange coming from a fashion stylist, but if you only take one thing away from this book, I hope it's the deep understanding that the power we get from what we wear is *always* about how the clothes make us *feel*.

A major reason I have found success in my calling as a fashion stylist is because I am laser-focused on making my clients feel how they desire to feel in any given moment—beautiful, glamorous, powerful, elegant—while also making them feel at ease in their own skin and in the second skin of their clothes. What could be more appealing? We are all seeking security in our embodied experience and the freedom to express ourselves and be who we truly are; we want to write our own stories dressed as our very best selves.

The issue is, when it comes to writing our own stories, a lot of us experience the style version of writer's block; I call it the "style stall out." The main, all-too familiar symptom: a closet full of clothes and nothing to wear, which leads to frustration and self-doubt and is the direct result of thinking what we desire is too far off, too big, too out of reach, or too something else. If you're one of those obstructed dreamers, I'm here to get you unblocked. I am very good at making the aspirational more accessible. As prolific self-help author and intuitive Laura Day says, "When you know your goal, intuition stops making you crazy and starts finding your opportunity."

So, what's *your* goal? What do you want to manifest in your life? How can you engage your intuition to help you accomplish that? And more importantly, how can you dress in a way that represents and summons the person you most want to be?

In the Introduction, I wrote that what I'm going to share with you is manifestation in fashion form. Here's a little more detail about what that means. Manifestation is the process of bringing your desires and intentions into reality by harnessing the power of your mind and beliefs. Feeling into what you want to happen before it happens is a cornerstone concept in manifestation. In Chapter 6 you'll be brought into how the brain accomplishes all of this when you hear from neuroscientist Dr. Tara Swart, who explains how adaptable our minds are and how the right "inputs" can change your reality in ways that seem too unreal to be scientific—but they are. These profound changes can be chalked up, scientifically, to something called neuroplasticity, our brain's remarkable ability to form new pathways at any point in our lives. In other words, we have the power to activate the life change we so desire.

Manifestation begins with envisioning who you want to be and then embodying that vision and believing it with your whole heart. Dressing the part, so to speak, works to help create the reality you desire. But using clothes as a life catalyst involves a lot more than just that.

Which brings us back to your closet. I have worked with all kinds of people and this "What the eff am I going to wear?" quandary keeps surfacing.

I started mentally cataloging why we're so confused, why it's so damn difficult to choose what to wear. See if any (or all) of the explanations on this list ring true for you:

Your wardrobe has become a time capsule, filled with pieces that reflect past selves: professional suits, skirts, and blouses from a corporate career (or clothes left over from any job at all that had specific wardrobe needs). The single-girl getups you wore for dates, or maternity and postnatal clothes, or way too much athleisure from years of working remotely. This last example is a fairly recent phenomenon, but it's taken hold. Recently, a friend told me this "athleisure wardrobe" topic came up in a focus group she attended and some of the ladies around the table admitted that up to seventy percent of their closets were comprised of comfy clothes, which seemed high. I'm not judging, but if that percentage doesn't work for your current life or your self-esteem and it's just become the default way to dress, then it's not working, period.

You got sucked into the trend algorithm, seduced by the steady stream of influencer content in your social feeds or by targeted clothing ads that beckoned you with that so-easy-to-click "buy" button—or, worse, the "after pay" option! Each of these "buy now, regret later" purchases represents a moment when you prioritized external pressure over internal wisdom. It happens all the time without us even realizing it.

A talented salesperson talked you into a style. Even well-meaning friends and partners sometimes convince you to take something home that just isn't you. You may have known it at the time, but you outsourced your judgment, and now you have things taking up space that had no business being there in the first place. If the tags are still on or you only wore the item once or twice, give them a second chance to make someone else happy by consigning or donating them.

You were under the travel spell. For me, nothing provides a dopamine hit like shopping in a distant place. I've lost count of how many times I have been so seduced by the beauty, romance, and sensory delight of a vacation spot that I've bought clothes that have a lot more to do with extending the feeling that location evokes than with how those pieces will actually function in my life. I mean, I don't exactly walk around photo shoots or sit at the computer in my office dressed in Grecian caftans (though the visual drama of it sounds kinda fab). Some people shop for real estate while on holiday; I shop for the wardrobe that makes me feel something new, invigorating, or exotic. But the reality is, it doesn't always translate once I get home.

It was a big-ticket item you feel guilty about. If you've ever dropped a chunk of money on a designer bag, coat, or other piece, then chances are you still have it—whether you've worn the item or not. It's hard to part with a fashion investment because for many of us, there is financial guilt involved in "treating" ourselves to something pricey. That's doubly true if we didn't actually enjoy the thing we bought. So there it hangs.

By the way, none of us is immune to the guilt associated with making expensive purchases, especially ones we don't get any mileage out of. Recently, I was talking with one of my clients, Mariska Hargitay, about this very topic. You may be familiar with Mariska, an actress, producer, and director, from her Emmy- and Golden Globe–winning portrayal of detective Olivia Benson on *Law & Order: Special Victims Unit*, or from her advocacy work for survivors of sexual assault and domestic violence through her Joyful Heart Foundation.

Mariska, also a mom of three, is so thoughtful about everything she does. So it was no surprise to me when she confessed even she has a hard time letting herself off the hook for fashion indulgences. "It's that thing about giving myself permission to let go, even though I had never worn this Chloé dress that was super expensive," Mariska told me, adding, "You have all that noise in your head." With a little nudging, Mariska found a solution that freed her from this burden of guilt. She gifted a few dresses she either hadn't worn or had only worn once to her sisters, along with these words: "You have that energy." By passing on her designer pieces (and the loving energy they carry) to family members she knew would *actually* enjoy them, Mariska cast off both the physical and the psychological weight they carried.

You're not that size anymore. And whether that size is bigger or smaller, you're probably not going back there. Each of those unwearable pieces carries emotional weight—fear, longing, shame. And they are a daily reminder of the gap between what might happen and what is.

Your interior truth is misaligned with your outward behavior. On a more erudite level, sometimes we betray our interior truth with our outward behavior, including the clothes we buy or hold on to. There are many reasons for this disharmony—external pressures and societal expectations, for starters. To cope with this, we rationalize our choices and convince ourselves that we are on the right path, even if it doesn't align with our deepest desires or self-image. Most, if not all, of us are conditioned to do this from a young age. In her book *On Our Best Behavior*, bestselling author Elise Loehnen offers an explanation. She says many women have "acquired personalities"—a set of habits and strategies they've developed to navigate the world. Elise, who also collaborated on *True and False Magic* with renowned psychotherapist Phil Stutz, writes that these chosen survival strategies are, on some level, normal or even healthy. However, if you become overly identified with this acquired personality or it becomes the sole way of engaging with the world, it can disconnect you from your truth.

This extends beyond behavior into how we dress. Elise says cultural trends "sent down runways to mass retailers and to magazines created an acquired personality writ large." She recounted her own experience as an editor in her twenties when she was trying to be a "fashion person" but had no idea what she was doing.

"I was test-driving all sorts of things, wearing all these trends," says Elise. "When I look back, my body was great, but even so, I looked like a buffoon." The past wardrobe we shed "becomes a trigger library," says Elise, only half joking. One that fits that category for her was a TV-personality wardrobe—clothes she thought she had to wear for television appearances: "bright colors like royal blue, which I didn't even own."

When I was living in Los Angeles, Elise and I would run into each other from time to time, usually just in passing, so I was thrilled to get to spend more than a few minutes with her during our interview. We chatted one afternoon via Zoom. I was in a conference room at the midtown Manhattan headquarters of Carolina Herrera, where I was doing a fitting with my client Anne Hathaway for her Met Gala look. Elise was in her car. It's a running joke that Los Angelinos live in their cars thanks to the infamous LA traffic—but in this case, Elise was simply escaping the hushed coworking space she writes from. Women just do whatever it takes to get the job done, right?

I asked her to say more about acquired personalities, because we can't dress with intention if we're dressing for a projected or internalized version of who we *think* we are. Elise told me, "Feeling free to broaden our behavioral and emotional repertoire—to not adhere so rigidly to our acquired personalities—is essential for personal growth and happiness." She's the first to admit this is not necessarily reflexive; it requires introspection and vigilant self-awareness. That way, when you catch yourself slipping into an acquired personality, you can adjust. It's incredibly common to act in ways that please other people. Women often do this by default. This is not pathology; it's societal conditioning, and it's not your fault. The great news is these behaviors can be unlearned as we anchor ourselves in our authentic self, and put away the acquired versions.

Elise has effectively jettisoned her acquired fashion personalities. She says she now prefers "a utilitarian, functional, well-tailored, high-quality piece of clothing" and shops perhaps once a year, buying only "five things that are new that are fresh and then I just wear them constantly." This shift broke "that spell" of compulsive buying, which she recognized in her thirties as an act of self-soothing. "I acquire very little and I wear what I buy over and over and over," she says.

Another key aspect of her current approach is refusing to wear anything that makes her "monitor my body. I don't want to be wearing something that's riding up that I'm pulling down. I don't want to feel like my stomach is exposed or not taut," she says. "I just can't do that anymore. I don't want to think about my body in that way ever again."

Moving beyond aspects of personality that were foisted on us comes down to becoming conscious of these conditioned patterns, whether behavioral or sartorial, and then choosing something different—choosing the message *you* want to convey. Says Elise: "It doesn't matter whether you think you care about clothing or not— you are creating. You're always telling a story about who you are."

Stutz's work, Elise says, emphasizes that the foundation of your life force starts with your relationship with your body. In that sense, it "valorizes how you dress your body, how you take care of your body—what's loving to your body."

Dr. Joe Dispenza, a bestselling author and lecturer known for his work on the mind-body connection and research on meditation, neuroscience, and healing, argues that becoming conscious of unconscious programs is the initiation to personal change. He explains, "Ninety-five percent of who we are is [the result of] those unconscious programs."[1] Therefore, creating a new life and a new reality for yourself requires becoming conscious of the automatic behaviors, routines, and emotional reactions that we've been conditioned into.

I wanted to know when this "programming" really gets baked in because, while no parent is perfect, I want to do whatever is possible to avoid messing up my kids! Here's a snapshot of what I learned: The most formative, crucial years are from birth to around age seven when the brain builds the neural foundation that will essentially determine how we see and react to the world for the rest of our lives.[2] In those early years, synapses (the learning and memory connections) are forming at up to one million per second.[3] Think about that: one million connections every single second. Equally fascinating is that after this initial burst, the brain starts pruning—systematically eliminating underutilized connections while strengthening the pathways that get used repeatedly. Essentially, the brain is saying "use it or lose it."

Unsurprisingly, what happens between caregivers (usually parents) and kids during these impressionable years has effects that ripple out far beyond childhood and impact our emotions, social skills, self-esteem, independence, how we handle stress, and so on. MRI studies now prove that the quality of our earliest experiences doesn't just influence us—those experiences become embedded in our brain's architecture.

No wonder changing deeply rooted patterns as adults takes *intentional* work. We have to go off autopilot and start consciously reinforcing the person we want to be instead of just operating as the person we were conditioned to be.

So, in order to figure out what the eff to wear, you first have to figure out who the eff you are—the *real* you. It goes without saying that figuring out who you are is a deep and lifelong pursuit. But doing a behavior audit can help you identify and unwind from deficits in your childhood development and social conditioning so you can get to the core of who you are or would like to become.

How to Do an Acquired Personality Audit

Through exercises that allow for self-observation, you can cultivate what pioneering psychologist Jon Kabat-Zinn calls "mindful awareness" of your automatic patterns.[4] This creates space between a stimulus, trigger, or environmental circumstance and your response, allowing you to make a conscious (and potentially different) choice about how to act.

Here are a handful of ways to get better at spotting your own patterns of behavior:

Keep a detailed "trigger log" of moments when you experience strong emotional reactions. Note the specific trigger, your immediate thought, your physical response, and your behavioral reaction. Pay particular attention to situations where your response seems disproportionate to the actual event, as these often reveal deeply conditioned patterns.

Document patterns, such as "When someone questions my work, I immediately feel defensive and become argumentative." This exercise helps identify what psychologist Albert Ellis called "irrational beliefs" that drive automatic behavioral responses.[5] I started doing this in work situations and it became clear when I was taking feedback personally, unnecessarily. I'm not alone—so many creatives take constructive criticism to heart. But now, with this zoomed-out view, I can see if I just listen to the feedback with some emotional detachment, I can use it as inspiration to try something new. It's not only a relief; it can also be fun.

Ask three people who know you well to describe your most predictable behavioral patterns, particularly in challenging situations. Compare their observations with your self-perception. Often, others can identify our conditioned responses more clearly because they observe us from outside our internal narrative, revealing blind spots in self-awareness. As psychologist Timothy Wilson notes in *Strangers to Ourselves*, we often lack conscious access to the mental processes that drive our behavior, making external feedback crucial for accurate self-assessment.[6]

My husband pointed out that, in conflict, I have an avoidance mechanism (not just with him!). I am supremely able to compartmentalize. While this may be useful as a survival mechanism—managing work travel with other responsibilities like a robot—it's not always the healthiest way to handle stressful situations. Since becoming more aware of when I slip into these avoidance patterns, I'm getting better at stopping to process my feelings instead of just automatically setting them aside.

Record yourself in conversations and play it back later to pick up on your speech patterns, interruption habits, or defense mechanisms. See if you notice anything you didn't realize was happening in the moment. (Always get consent to record from the person you're speaking with.)

Once you've gathered data from multiple exercises, look for recurring themes across different contexts. Conditioned patterns typically cluster around core psychological needs: control, approval, security, or achievement. For instance, you might notice that whether you're at work, in relationships, or facing personal challenges, you consistently prioritize others' approval over your preferences.

These pattern clusters often trace back to adaptive strategies developed early in life that may no longer serve your current circumstances. The goal is not necessarily to eliminate all conditioned responses—some serve useful functions—but to bring them into conscious awareness so you can choose when to engage or override them.

Set pattern-breaking challenges for yourself. Decide in advance how you might respond differently than your default, and challenge yourself to do just that. A few examples to try:

- The next time someone compliments you or your work, just try a simple "thank you" instead of downplaying it. See how it feels to just own the praise. I am one to remind friends and clients (even strangers) to just accept rather than deflect a compliment—graciously of course—as an offering of self-compassion.
- Many of us dance around what we actually need by prefacing requests with qualifiers. Politely saying to an assertive salesperson, "I'd like to see this dress in black before deciding" feels different energetically than "I was just wondering if perhaps it might be possible to see some other options before I decide—if you have time to show me."
- If you always speak first in a meeting or are always the one to find

the solution to a problem, try hanging back. Ask a question and then *really* listen—not just waiting for your turn to chime in but actually taking in what other people are saying. Quieter friends, coworkers, spouses (and kids, for that matter) often have gold to share, if you give them a little space. And it might be nice to test what it feels like to rescind the responsibility of being the fixer.

✗ Ever catch yourself reflexively stepping aside when someone walks toward you in a room? Try holding your ground next time. Not in an aggressive way—just occupying your territory unapologetically. It's a small thing that feels surprisingly powerful.

✗ Here's an example of something that I needed to adjust in myself: I noticed that I was overly attentive around certain people; I would try to cater to their every need. And it wasn't because I was being asked outright to do this. I just somehow sensed that there was an expectation of me to act that way. For me, breaking a pattern like this requires a little magical thinking. Yes, I believe in magic—and I practice it, too! Nothing too witchy. But I do find it helpful to harness energetic principles of protection at times I need to feel a little shielded. So when I feel compelled to overextend myself to please another person, here are some energy tools I silently use in the moment to create a nice buffer or boundary:

✗ **Light shield:** Visualizing a protective cocoon of white light surrounding my entire body. I like this one—it feels very Harry Potter–esque.

✗ **Growing roots:** Imagining tree roots extending from my feet deep into the earth is anchoring and stabilizing.

✗ **Waterfall cleansing:** Picturing purifying water flowing over me, washing away other people's emotions or expectations.

✗ **Crossing my arms or legs:** This is a subtle way to create an energetic boundary in challenging conversations. The other person *never* suspects a thing, but *you* feel more secure.

✗ **Putting a hand on my heart:** When feeling pulled into someone else's emotional state it helps to connect with my own heart center. I do this one a lot.

✗ **Purse-or-pocket talismans:** Carrying a black stone (such as obsidian or tourmaline, which are thought to absorb or deflect negative energy) or a crystal (such as selenite or rose quartz) can serve as tangible reminders of unseen support. It can also be *any* stone. Just the other day I picked up a stone at the beach with my young son. He was having a tough day, so I told him he could hold it when he was feeling frustrated or upset. I could see the shift, the relief on his face just knowing he had this little trick, if not up his sleeve then at least in his pocket.

✗ **Zipping up:** Imagining myself closing an energetic zipper from my feet to the top of my head. Leave it to a fashion person to find an apparel-like tool!

✗ **Returning to sender:** Mentally releasing energy that doesn't belong to you back to wherever it came from. I do this daily at the end of the day by silently asking the universal powers that be to "release the energy that is not mine." I feel it instantly.

You'll hear much more about energy alignment and how to leverage its power in Chapter 6.

Regularly expose yourself to diverse perspectives through reading, conversations, or experiences that challenge your default worldview. I find that growing your knowledge base and enriching your life in these ways is fundamental to getting in touch with your highest self. When you live inside an echo chamber of people and ideas that mirror yours, there is very little room for questioning why you do what you do. Be open to listening without trying to change someone's mind. I know that's especially hard in a world where political and personal views are so polarized. To me, it's more important (and a lot less aggravating) to attempt to understand where someone is coming from rather than try to convince them to change.

Seek therapy with a professional trained in cognitive behavioral approaches who can help identify unconscious patterns. There are now so many online services that make finding a therapist easier and less expensive. And, I hope, less stigmatized. Therapy is a form of self-exploration and care. It may not be for everybody, but it's definitely an avenue to consider.

Notice physical sensations that accompany emotional reactions. Body awareness can signal when you're slipping into reactive patterns. Maybe your face flushes or your stomach lurches or your eyes well up or you feel a shooting pain in your temple. Not too long ago I was listening to singer Miley Cyrus being interviewed on a podcast. She said that earlier in her career, when she didn't feel emotionally safe or was in a situation where she didn't feel she could speak up for herself, her throat tightened up. That tracks— she's a singer and her throat is where she feels everything, both good and bad. Many of us have a "spot" like that—a physical area that communicates more loudly than the rest of our bodies. What might be yours?

Many cultures, religions, and other ancient wisdom traditions, such as Hinduism and Buddhism, attribute certain physical ailments to destabilizations in the chakra system—the seven energy centers that run vertically through your body and represent gateways where your emotional life, your spiritual essence, and your physical reality converge. Each chakra, it is believed, governs specific organs and systems. For example, your heart chakra doesn't just process love; it correlates to your cardiovascular and respiratory systems. Years of unexpressed grief can show up as asthma or heart disease. Your root chakra anchors your immune system and foundational stability. When this center holds unhealed trauma around safety or belonging, your body responds through immune dysfunction or persistent lower back pain. If I ever doubted this connection, it vanished when my friend Michele ended up having to have back surgery because the disc located between her L5, S1 vertebrae at the base—or root—of the spine gave out just a few short months after her mother passed away. Our parents represent our foundation—our root—so experiencing this level of destabilization after such a loss makes sense to me.

I have my own physical "weakness" that may have an energetic component. I've struggled with epilepsy since I was a teenager. I take daily medication and will likely need to for the rest of my life. One energy healer I spoke to suggested that the convulsive activity of an epileptic seizure might have actually opened up my brain and body to be more intuitively receptive. While there is a rare form of epilepsy that's been linked with mystical experiences and increased awareness, I can't say whether my form has anything to do with a higher-functioning sense of intuition.[7] But I do like the idea that an ailment might also be a gift—and I certainly consider myself to be an intuitive, open person.

We'll go deeper into aligning the chakra system in Chapter 6.

But in general, I believe that gaining somatic self-understanding is crucial for informing our intuition and decisions.

Our bodies are the ultimate TRUTH TELLERS. We just need to TUNE IN.

For me, it's often my gut. I feel knots and twists in my stomach if I am presented with an idea, proposal, person, or anything that doesn't feel like it's in alignment with my personal truth. It's gotten to the point that I can't even answer or write an email or text without my gut directing me first.

I'm not alone in this. The gut is often referred to as the "second brain" due to its complex network of neurons and its significant role in processing our emotions, intuition, and even decision-making. It contains millions of nerve cells and communicates bidirectionally with the brain, influencing mood and mental states—in other words, it's a two-way street. Your gut is rich in receptors and neurotransmitters, such as serotonin, which are also found in the brain, and these play a crucial role in how we experience intuition—aka "gut feelings." That term makes even more sense now, right? This biologically rooted connection explains why emotions can trigger physical sensations in the belly and why it is so closely linked to our instinctive reactions.

Shadow Work in Your Closet

Another hidden influence that works behind the scenes to form our self-picture and map our behavior patterns pertains to our so-called shadow side. Let me explain what the concept means from a psychological standpoint. Famed Swiss psychiatrist Carl Jung theorized that the shadow self represents the part of our psyche that holds everything we don't want to acknowledge about ourselves—concealed dimensions that include emotions, traits, and desires we've tucked away from conscious awareness because they're too uncomfortable, shameful, or contrary to our ideal self-image. Just a few examples of these traits: egocentricity, secretiveness, jealousy, envy, sexual identity, perfectionism, rage, sexism, emotional detachment, lustfulness—the list goes on and on because, while there are areas that are commonly involved in "shadow" traits (money, sex, power), it really comes down to how the individual judges their inner truth.

Sort of like the clothes you've hidden in the back of your closet, your shadow contains the stories you don't tell, the feelings you suppress, and sometimes even the positive qualities you've denied. These aspects may be buried but trust me, they still influence how you move through the world.

"Shadow work" refers to anything you do to confront these hidden influences of yourself. Engagement could be informal, such as noticing repeating relationship patterns or triggers. Or more formal, such as working with a Jungian-trained analyst or doing an intensive program, such as the famous Hoffman Process, which focuses on those aforementioned patterns inherited from parents and caregivers that operate unconsciously in your adult life. These are deeper dives, but all of us can benefit from bringing our shadow side into awareness in the intentional pursuit of growth. I bring up all these avenues of self-exploration simply to expose the various ways we can get cozier with the parts of ourselves that we feel compelled to keep hidden.

By the way, shadow work doesn't necessarily aim to eliminate your shadow side (unless it is truly harming you or others), but rather to integrate it so that you're more empowered to express yourself authentically. I love the term *integrate* because to me it connotes healthy acceptance. The word *shadow* sounds kind of sinister, but it isn't typically something to fear. Just think of it as one piece of your unique personal puzzle.

In a way, I have always seen myself as more of a fashion therapist than a fashion stylist. In the past I struggled with the label "celebrity stylist" because it didn't seem to capture the depth of what I consider my calling to be. I want to help anyone I work with become their highest, best self—using clothes. I want them to feel seen, and style has the unique power to accomplish that. I also want them to feel more whole, and wholeness becomes more possible when you feel seen and comfortable and authentic in what you're wearing. It *is* fashion therapy.

Actress Kerry Washington, who is just such an exquisite human, shared a story with me that perfectly illustrates how clothes can shift your emotional state. "I'm working these long hours right now, and I'm missing my family," admitted Kerry, who was in the middle of filming *Imperfect Women* when we chatted. "So I wore my husband's concert T-shirt today because I can feel close to this person that I love on a day when I'm sad to be leaving the house at 4:30 a.m." Kerry rocking a '90s summer vibe in an oversized tee and cute shorts while *also* proactively, *intentionally* picking an outfit that helped her feel closer to her husband is a major style win in my book—and hers.

Take it from Kerry: Going beyond the surface elements of fashion and style doesn't have to be complicated. And by the time you get to the end of this book, you will be your own fashion therapist, *if* you're down to get real with yourself. To ask more of yourself every day. To evolve and keep evolving. By shedding the programming and expectations that often take over and instead relying on our intuition to guide us, the clothes we choose become tools for stepping into our authentic selves. The way I see it, when we open our closets in the morning, we're confronted with the opportunity to either reinforce or gently challenge how we thought we should dress, act, live.

I remember a handful of years ago, I was at the home of one of my regular clients, sitting on the floor of her large, pristine bathroom organizing the accessories I would use to style her. I was lining up rows of colored pumps, glam handbags, and baguettes and trays of glittering jewelry when I looked up and saw that she was watching me. "Erin, how long will you be doing this?" she asked. She didn't want to know how much longer I'd be there, crouched down on her marble tile. She was hinting that I had more to offer than just arranging shoes and bags—or even styling. I instinctively knew that, too. I knew that I wanted to take what I was perceiving as a stylist—specifically the ability of clothing to summon your higher self and propel your life forward—and articulate it as a mindset and a method that anyone (everyone!) could benefit from.

I couldn't have begun the process that would end up being this book without *consciously* choosing to evolve, without questioning my motivations, and without actively expanding my job description. I was already successful by industry standards. I could have left it at that. But the GPS of my soul was formulating a reroute.

I sought the answer to this question: *Did I have something meaningful to say about the deeper relationship between style and self-worth?* It took months to recognize the pattern—a high percentage of my styling jobs turned into impromptu personal mini-transformation sessions. So yes, these insights deserved a broader platform—a book, a podcast, a movement. Still, I had to confront my concern about being seen as "just" a fashion expert even though I'd been upgrading lives one wardrobe at a time for years. I finally decided I was ready to expand my box of career possibilities by exploring style as a means of self-discovery. My unique perspective was not only valid; it was necessary. To expand, I had to be vulnerable. The alternative was staying small when I knew I had more to offer. As my friend Marie Forleo always says: "There has never been and never will be another you. You have a purpose—a very special gift that only you can bring to the world." Marie is a phenomenal business coach, motivational speaker, podcast host, and author of the number one *New York Times* bestseller *Everything Is Figureoutable*. She shares her tips for gaining clarity on your desires in the next chapter.

False or outdated beliefs about ourselves show up in our wardrobes because so often, we're following external rules. We're staying small. Maybe it's the belief that we always need to look professional to be taken seriously, or pulled together, or to appear demure or, conversely, provocative and sexy. Liberation comes when we recognize these constraints are self-imposed; they aren't absolutes or even truths. Who's making the rules anyway? You're the boss of you, and that includes calling the shots about your style choices.

To start feeling into the life we want, we need to take action in alignment with our deeper truths. We can gain all of the self-awareness in the world, but then we have to do something with that newfound information. That's where our clothing choices can become a daily action we take to honor our truth beneath those layers of conditioning.

No one is a bigger proponent of taking action than intuitive expert and bestselling author Laura Day, whose work has influenced billion-dollar business leaders, celebrities, and thousands of students seeking to harness their intuitive abilities. Laura is a groundbreaking thinker when it comes to tuning in to your inner life and authentic self. Her newest book, *The Prism*, offers a system for understanding, healing, and working with the seven ego centers—her term for the seven energy centers of the chakra system.

I'm not prone to hyperbole, but my mind was blown when I got to speak with Laura for this book. She was in London with her husband, and I was at a summer rental in Montauk—the farthest town on Long Island's east end—with my family. There must have been divine forces supporting our teleconferencing that day because, against all odds, it worked without a glitch. Laura began by telling me that the real difference between most self-help and the style she proposes is that hers "isn't about just continuing to look inside yourself because if all the answers were there, you would have answered the questions. It's about doing something small and safe differently and noticing how the world encounters and responds to you."

Our clothing choices, I believe, represent one of the most accessible ways to practice this action-based alignment, and I was eager to hear Laura's POV. She agreed, emphasizing that we need to move beyond dressing on autopilot and ask ourselves questions such as "What am I signaling to myself?" and "What am I signaling to the world?"

The key, according to Laura, is learning to read the feedback from our environment: "One of the biggest mistakes that I see in my new students is that they wear things they *think* are sending a certain message instead of noticing the reactions from the world to what they're wearing. The reaction they assume or anticipate they'll get is often wrong."

I love Laura's suggestion to make subtle, safe adjustments to style choices and then observe how the world responds. (She had many more insights to share about how to use your intuition to power your style choices. You'll encounter those gems throughout the book.)

This disconnect between intention and reception is something I often encounter when working with clients. I like to factor in one more element: how the person wants to be *remembered*. For instance, a client might feel amazing and sexy when they try on a super-revealing dress to wear the night of their movie's premiere. But if that event is just one night in a series that will be part of an awards campaign aimed at highlighting the actor's increasing gravitas and ability to take on more complex roles, I might advise against it. Don't get me wrong, sometimes a dress that slays is exactly what's called for. (Hello, Elizabeth Hurley's safety pin dress and JLo's plunging Versace number, two examples of sexy-statement gold that are still memorable over twenty-five years later.) But a barely there gown *might not* be the best choice if sexy is the actor's default vibe and what people expect. It won't help move the needle to a new place for that person's image and career.

Of course, to Laura Day's point, this analysis is based on having some data points to pull from—such as knowing the history of how the "environment" (audience) responds to the look. Changing the look provides an opportunity for a new data point (reaction) to emerge and build on. Small, safe changes.

Granted, we don't all have huge audiences to pull data from like celebrities do, but we don't need to. You can gain this understanding from anyone you encounter: your spouse, friends, colleagues, fellow partygoers, and strangers you pass on the street.

In the next chapter, I will share tools that will help you unearth your authentic wants and needs because my guess is you've outgrown more than just certain styles or sizes, or even acquired personalities. You've outgrown the torment of not knowing what the eff to wear and why you find it so difficult to get dressed. And further, what you're *really* seeking, beneath all the fabric and all those fashion rules, is a sense of peace—the kind that only comes when your outer expression aligns with your inner truth. And from where I sit, peace is the low bar. I want you to have that as a given, as a starting point. And then I want you to have a lot more. I want you to have all of the excitement, contentment, optimism, and, yes, serenity that you desire.

Chapter Summary

Threading It All Together

The struggle with "what the eff to wear" isn't about lacking clothes or style—it's about misalignment between your inner truth and outer expression. Your closet has likely become a museum of past selves and pieces acquired to meet external expectations rather than internal desires. From birth to age seven, your brain embedded patterns that still shape how you see yourself today—unconscious programming running on autopilot. But neuroplasticity means your brain can form new pathways at any point.

Quick Alterations to Make

X **Document your patterns.** Capture emotional reactions—the trigger, thoughts, physical responses, and behavior. Awareness is the foundation of change.

X **Get outside perspectives.** Ask trusted people to describe your predictable patterns and compare them with your self-perception. These insights reveal blind spots.

X **Break one pattern this week.** Accept a compliment with just "thank you," make a direct request without qualifiers, or let someone else speak first in a meeting. Notice how liberating it feels to respond differently.

X **Question the rules.** Each morning, challenge external expectations by asking: "Whose voice is guiding my choices— mine or someone else's? What am I signaling to myself and the world?"

X **Experiment and observe.** Make small style adjustments, then observe how people actually respond rather than assuming the message you're sending. Gather real data.

Continue Designing Your Future

✗ **Develop energetic boundaries through visualization.** Imagine protective white light shields, grounding tree roots from your feet, or place a hand on your heart when you feel pulled to overextend. Carry talismans as tangible reminders of your commitment to honoring your energy.

✗ **Integrate your shadow self.** Accept hidden aspects as pieces of your unique puzzle. This integration allows you to dress from wholeness rather than fragmentation.

Ultimately, you're building toward peace as your baseline—the kind that flows when your outer expression aligns with your inner truth. Dressing to create the reality you envision transforms getting dressed from a source of stress into an act of self-empowerment.

Practical Magic

INTRODUCING THE **CREATE** METHOD

"I think that what we're seeking
is an experience of being alive,
so that our life experiences
on the purely physical plane
will have resonances with our
own innermost being and
reality, so that we actually feel
the rapture of being alive."

JOSEPH CAMPBELL

I've admitted that I believe in a certain kind of magic. But there was a point in time when we *all* believed in it. We got excited about getting dressed—or rather, dressing up. Our closets were those portals to possibility.

It was when we were children, of course. Back then, we were able to approach dress-up time with joy, transforming into princesses or explorers (or zoo animals, for that matter) without hesitation or self-judgment. Dressing up was acknowledged as a creative outlet. It was encouraged. And we weren't afraid of what people might think of our choices—whether those choices included a wedding dress, tiara, police badge, or furry tail. Each costume change was an adventure waiting to happen—a gateway to a different and potentially magical place.

Somewhere along the way this joyful activity morphs into something a lot less fun. The mirror, once our ally in transformation, becomes the lens through which our inner critic has its clearest view. (Think Demi Moore's destructive self-view in the movie *The Substance,* where her character—a celebrity fitness instructor—takes extreme measures to maintain her youth. It is a horror-esque take on how society's unattainably high beauty standards can have destructive consequences.)

I was curious about when this shift takes place, and I was shocked by what I discovered. Research shows that girls' negative self-perceptions start early. As they enter elementary school, their focus on looks intensifies, and when they hit their teens, appearance-related self-criticism really ramps up.[1] By late adolescence, many young women report constantly critiquing themselves about their bodies.[2] This breaks my heart. Sometimes this critical inner voice mirrors their mothers' or other influential female figures' own appearance anxieties, which is something I try to be super conscious of.

our closets were the portals to possibility

Not surprising, during middle school, high school, and college, cultural ideals and media (social media included) exposure heavily influence how young women view and present themselves. Many young women constantly monitor their appearance, which we know can negatively impact their body image.

Just typing this I feel exhausted thinking about how much energy is expended focusing on external pressures and unrealistic ideals during the course of the female lifespan. My fatigue is a great example of that somatic signaling I was talking about earlier—the way your body tells you how you *really* feel. Part of what informs this feeling in me is that I remember going through these stages myself.

If any of this seems hypocritical given that I work in the fashion industry, just know that I exist to do things differently than what you might expect—or assume. I'm driven by the need to bring depth and purpose to fashion, which is so often viewed as a vapid industry, deservedly or not. More on that later.

This book is part of a larger mission I have to rearchitect how women see themselves, to rearchitect how *you* see yourself. The messages in these pages are ones I wish I'd received growing up. In the safe space of this book and the community and movement I want to create, I have to be completely honest. And raw. I have suffered for most of my life in varying degrees with body dysmorphia—that is, I have spent a lot of time worrying about flaws in my appearance. Technically, body dysmorphia is a mental health issue, but it is so pervasive, so commonplace, and so normalized in women that it barely registers as a problem to be addressed. I can trace mine back to age seven; age eight, especially, sticks out in my mind. I remember pinching the fat on my belly with my small fingers, wondering how I might change my shape, willing it to happen.

So like most women—and likely, most of you—I've spent countless hours over my lifetime, even as a fashion expert, wondering if something will make me look slim enough, or chic enough, or inspiring enough, or simply *enough*. I, too, have stared into my closet feeling at a loss despite all the tools at my disposal. But I finally got to a point where I'd had enough. Maybe you've had enough, too. So here we are, together.

This is a good place for me to stop and confess that this book isn't *just* for you. Or even you and me. It's also for my eleven-year-old daughter, Matilda, who is on the precipice of young womanhood. I recognize all of the hallmarks emerging. She is afraid and pretends not to be. She is beautiful and can't see it. She's even beginning to feel confused about what to wear! And like every other daughter on earth, she's not about to listen to her mom's spoken advice. So I'm writing.

All young women, my darling daughter included, need more role models in the world who still look at their closet as an enchanting place or who are willing to relearn how to view it that way. I hope every person who reads this book falls into one of those two categories because when you align your wardrobe with your essence—your authentic self that's yearning to emerge—getting dressed becomes a key ingredient in a larger process of self-development. That self-development is its own kind of fashion alchemy—the stylistic transformation that will lead to you feeling your best. Feeling the most *you*.

Before we go on, I also want to address any assumptions you may have about the stars I style. It's reasonable to think fame and affluence buffer you from the woes of the average woman—that having celebrity status means you have the means (money, access, etc.) to feel great about yourself. Money helps with a lot of things in life. But nobody feels great all the time, even with all the wealth and privilege in the world, because self-esteem always has more to do with inner well-being than anything you can buy to distract yourself from your interior truth. Sure, some people have more innate confidence or a greater capacity to filter out external noise. But even after you finish this book and master the principles I'm sharing, you still have to face the noise. Not just from the outside, but from within. We *all* have to do that, celebs included.

Actors and entertainers have critical inner voices, too—no matter how amazing they may look to you when you see them on a red carpet. I might even argue they have to contend with louder voices than most of us. That's a big reason it's been so rewarding to see the positive ripple effect my process has on my clients' inner and outer lives—it's a process they take an active part in. And because many of them have such high visibility, I hope working with them in the specific and intentional way that I do can have an amplifying effect.

Because you don't have to just admire this embodied way of dressing from afar—you can possess it.

To do that, I'm going to ask that you suspend your disbelief and embrace the idea that anything is possible for you. I get that some of you might approach anything too "woo-woo" with skepticism. I try to dispel some of that doubt with the scientific receipts on how this stuff works. But I'm not here to spout spiritual or fashion dogma; I'm simply inviting you to find your own process for using style as a tool of manifestation. Make this book your own.

When I was studying acting at NYU's Tisch School of the Arts, one of my acting teachers, the late and great Ron Burrus, handed each student a sheet of paper with this quote from American mythology writer Joseph Campbell typed on it: "I think that what we're seeking is an experience of being alive, so that our life experiences on the purely physical plane will have resonances with our own innermost being and reality, so that we actually feel the rapture of being alive."

Taking in that sentence felt more like remembering something than reading a quote for the first time. Perhaps I had intuited its essence before that moment. I hope this method conjures a similar feeling in you—a reunion with your inner magic so you can feel ignited by life's possibilities.

The language I choose to use to communicate the fashion magic I personally believe in starts with my core method of intentional dressing, easily remembered with the acronym **CREATE**.

It's your turn to go supernova.

Alchemy is transformation through mysterious or supernatural forces, and through the CREATE method, you can concoct your own powerful alchemy for change. In this case *you* are that supernatural force. As mega-designer Michael Kors once said to me during a Met Gala fitting with actress Kerry Washington, "Fashion is meant to make you feel like the supernova version of yourself."

So let's go supernova. Let's CREATE.

I'll walk you through what each step represents and then the following chapters will delve deeper into each one and how you can incorporate the information and practices into your own life.

CLARITY
: Getting clear is so important—both for tapping into how you want/need to feel on any given day and for zeroing in on your bigger dreams.

RITUAL
: Finding routines that ground you at the start of each day or whenever you need centering. Many of these will leverage the power of your senses.

EDITING
: Transforming your closet into creative fuel and possibility. Your wardrobe can become a curated library of feelings—and a portal to who you want to evolve into.

ALIGNMENT
: Harmonizing your physical and energetic bodies to make what you wear a cohesive force of change.

TRUTH
: Ensuring authenticity in how you present yourself to the world—and how you operate in it—is paramount. It's all about living in integrity.

EXPANSION
: Opening up to new possibilities, habits, and experiments with style will ensure your confidence and curiosity continues to grow.

CREATE provides the framework for developing how you want to feel and who you want to be. It's your means to manifest the life you want, with style. By the end of the last chapter, you'll know exactly how to do that.

One experience I had back at *Vogue* comes to mind just about every time I get dressed. I'll replay it for you: I had been the assistant on a shoot with Irving Penn, one of the most revered fashion photographers of all time. I had heard through the grapevine of the *Vogue* offices that Editor-in-Chief Anna Wintour had killed the shoot after reviewing the film. (In magazine parlance, this means that the images didn't make it into the issue.)

As I stood in the art department staring at the wall where small printouts of the images hung as part of the magazine's potential layout, I was surprised by the emotions I felt. It seemed sad to me that they'd never see the light of day—such a waste of creativity. I audaciously asked why the shoot was being killed. I just didn't get it. The explanation I remember being given boils down to this: When you look at a fashion story, you should "want to be that girl." And reportedly, Anna didn't think those particular Penn images would evoke that feeling. Penn reshot the story and that film did run! Still, I respect Anna's integrity, vision, and allegiance to her readers' needs.

That single experience taught me something vital and lasting about personal style: Each piece you choose should reflect the person you want to be. Not only that, but any discomfort you have with your current wardrobe is just a compass pointing toward the need for a new direction. Those moments of uncertainty are actually invitations to grow, to expand, and to realign your outer expression with your inner truth.

Unlocking what's behind our discontent—in this case, not knowing what to wear or not feeling great in your current style—is actually a sign something is ready to shift. I want your journey of self-discovery to evolve to a place where, when you look in the mirror, you want to be—as Anna so wisely put it—"that girl": liking how she looks and also how she feels, and what she is offering to the world. If imagining that level of contentment seems foreign, don't worry. I've been down this road many times with many people, so I'll guide the way using easy exercises, rituals, and routines to ground you in the feelings (key word!) of being your highest self.

I tend to like routines, rituals, and active exercises over simple affirmations because affirmations are often just statements or platitudes. They can be helpful in certain instances (and I do tap the "like" button when I see one that resonates with me on Instagram!), but they aren't always rooted in the *feelings* you need to conjure. I'm all about the feelings.

The first exercise I want to introduce is meant to exorcise self-loathing and self-criticism—the distorted self-perceptions that are ever present in so many women—and welcome self-acceptance and self-love. It's foundational.

To own who you are, you need to *see* who you are. You need to get comfortable with her, whether it's for a public appearance in front of millions, or just to face your partner at breakfast in the morning. When I'm with clients before an event, we don't just practice poses to see which angle works best for the camera. We do that, but we also summon self-compassion, gratitude, and love. Love conquers fear; any card-carrying spiritualist will tell you that. And trust me, any event becomes less scary when you love not only your outfit but the person wearing it.

Taking the time to see who you are and how you are feeling gives you insight into whether what you choose to wear will support you or not. This is essential, but I'm not going to lie: I don't always feel like staring at myself in the mirror and getting real—especially when I'm not feeling great in my body or I'm tired or anxious. More often than not, when I do this practice, it clarifies how I *feel*, which points to what I need to *wear* to get me to how I *want* to feel. It unites me, with intention, to the *woman I want to be.*

Morning Mirror Exercise

Give this a try to elevate your self-perception and return to the magical human you are.

WHAT YOU'LL NEED

X   5–7 minutes in the morning or whenever you need it
X   A full-length mirror
X   *Optional:* A centering scent—incense, essential oils, etc. (Detailed suggestions can be found in Chapter 4.)

Set the Scene
Stand in front of your mirror. If possible, light a candle, diffuse an

essential oil, or burn a small piece of palo santo or sage. Scent helps anchor you in the present moment.

Get Centered

Close your eyes and feel your feet firmly planted on the ground. Take at least three deep, slow breaths to activate the parasympathetic nervous system, which signals your body to relax.

Work Through the CALM Checklist

Open your eyes and look at your reflection. Gently place your hands on your heart and review these steps:

CLARITY: How do I want to feel today? (e.g., "I want to feel peaceful," "I want to feel powerful," "I want to feel creative.")

ASSESSMENT: Take a moment to *feel* that desired emotion in your body. For example: If your desired feeling is "I want to feel powerful," identify where strength or energy arises in your body—maybe in your core or legs. Focus on that area in your mind and breathe deeply into it, feeling your power expand.

LOVE: Send love and acknowledgment to your reflection, exactly as you are. At first this might feel odd or foreign, but trust me, it works wonders. Simply say: "I love you and I support you."

MANTRA: Choose a simple mantra that cements your desired feeling (e.g., "Peace flows through me," "I am a vessel of creativity," "I am strong and capable"). Even a well-known slogan such as "Keep Calm and Carry On" does the trick for me when I have to keep many balls in the air. Repeat it aloud three times.

Enter the Portal

To finish, look back in the mirror, which is now a portal. See not just your reflection, but the person you are actively becoming through your intentional choices.

Seal the Practice

Express gratitude for this opportunity to align. Say to yourself: "I am ready to magnetize all that is meant for me." Notice how different you feel.

If you do this mirror exercise daily for a week it will start to feel instinctive and the effort it takes will diminish. It's meant to jump-start the process of honoring yourself. At this point, I don't need to do it every single day, but I return to it when I need to press pause.

There are certain concepts in this book that will echo throughout the pages—such as getting vulnerable enough to listen to your own heart. I find that even just running through the CALM checklist alone is a helpful way to tap into optimistic, heart-centered energy.

You might be wondering, *"Erin, but what about the clothes???"* I promise you, nothing is going to make sense *on* your body until you confront your relationship with it. Actively shifting your self-perception to one of embrace instead of insult will alter the way you view getting dressed.

The style advice is coming—don't you worry!

Sara Blakely

You might know Sara Blakely as the pioneering creator of Spanx shapewear and first among the world's youngest self-made female billionaires. But beyond her incredible business success lies a powerful story of manifesting a life aligned with deep purpose.

I'd never met Sara in person until I interviewed her for this book. But I knew from following her on social media that Sara is very into manifestation practices. And I wanted to hear it *all*. We met up at the chic WSA building in lower Manhattan where I have an office, when she was in New York City to celebrate one of her sons' birthdays. I felt an immediate sisterhood with Sara. We're both native Floridians, busy moms, fashion innovators—and committed manifesters. I wanted to talk to Sara all day because she had so many interesting and useful things to say, but since she had a tight timeline I focused on getting the intel on how, exactly, she made her very big dreams a reality.

For anyone out there who feels lost, you should know that Sara didn't start out with a clear path. In her twenties, she was unsure what she wanted to do. She thought about becoming a lawyer but bombed the LSAT—twice. She auditioned to be Goofy at Disney World, but alas, you have to be 5'8" and she is only 5'6". She landed a sales job peddling fax machines, which she did for a decade!

All the while, though, she was consciously investing in her self-development and that investment paid off, figuratively and literally. Here is what she shared with me about how to call in your desires.

1. Invest in your mindset.

Investing in your internal world is a critical first step toward external creation. Even when Sara didn't know her ultimate direction, she spent every spare second listening to spiritual and motivational speakers such as Wayne Dyer, Tony Robbins, Zig Ziglar, and Brian Tracy. "I became so hungry for mindset development and the lessons of these teachers changed the trajectory of my life completely," says Sara.

For starters, it helped her navigate uncertainty without excessive worry because she began to trust that she would figure things out when the time was right. If you're curious but feel a bit timid about exploring these ideas, you can start by just using Instagram. Follow the accounts of spiritual teachers, self-help leaders, Human Design experts, and more, such as Gabrielle Bernstein, Esther Abraham-Hicks, Paulo Coelho, Lewis Howes, Mel Robbins, Shaman Durek, Jenna Zoe, Yung Pueblo, and others. I recently added Emma Grede, a mega-successful fashion business entrepreneur, to the list. I am loving her practical take on spiritual and *big* ideas—and that she generously shares actionable ideas for incorporating her wisdom into your own life.

Take a little time to see what resonates with you. And do some cursory research on the people behind the accounts: Look to see who else follows them, if they've written books, been featured on panels or invited to speak at established institutions, cited in industry forums, or interviewed by reputable outlets.

2. Set specific intentions.

Sara's breakthrough moment came after a tough day selling fax machines. She went home and wrote this in her journal: "I will invent my own product that I can sell to millions of people that will make them feel good." This wasn't a vague wish; it was a clear, affirmative written declaration of intention, made two years before the Spanx idea was born. It was specific.

Once she had set the intention to invent a product, Sara didn't just passively wait around. She actively engaged with the process of *receiving* the idea. "I asked the universe very specifically, 'Give me the idea. I don't know what it is, but when you give it to me, I will not squander it,'" remembers Sara. When she recounted this, I got chills thinking about how meaningful that single request would become.

That's the thing about Sara: She isn't afraid to ask for what she needs—repeatedly. To this day, she implores the universe to guide her by saying: "I need a sign. I need it to be really specific, and preferably before Wednesday." Ha! Sara says: "This opens the door for the universe to respond."

I wholeheartedly believe in asking for guidance and have been doing it myself for years—which, for a while, meant enduring some teasing from my Swedish husband who is not wired to put stock in such unconventional practices. But over the years he's witnessed the power of operating from an intention-driven mindset as I've manifested everything from brand collaborations to clients I wanted to work with to coast-to-coast moves where I've found the perfect homes for our brood in some of the most competitive real estate markets. At this point, he has little choice but to relent and admit that there is actually "something to it."

3. Make space to hear the downloads.

Intuition is a vital superpower. At some point, Sara realized she could best access these inner nudges (or "downloads," as she refers to them) when she was alone. She said that rote activities, like driving, are particularly conducive for her. Since these days Sara's office is close to home, she builds in a "fake commute" by driving aimlessly around her Atlanta suburb to give herself space to daydream and receive insights. This is the first time I have ever heard of someone intentionally extending their commute, but Sara does things differently and that's the point!

She also takes solo vacations or "think vacations," saying: "Thanks to our phones, all of the allowing of space is gone—but it's in the space that we get creative and tap into our intuition."

Since I already travel so much for work, I haven't yet been able to negotiate a "think vacation" with my husband. So until my kids get a bit older and I can manage a real getaway, I've applied the wisdom imparted to me by Laura Day to see every moment of the day as a ritual. With that in mind, I take "mini think vacations" in the middle of the day when my schedule permits or just when I really need one. If I get stuck or frustrated on set and need to take a beat to regain my creative styling flow, I'll walk to the nearest coffee bar or even just to the bathroom to take a few deep breaths. After moving from LA to New York City, I relish living in such a pedestrian-oriented city— walking is often how you get places here, so I use that time to let my mind wander, too. Fashion designer Diane von Fürstenberg told me she swims for two hours almost every day to activate her mind and summon clarity. *J'adore*, though I don't think I could swim for two hours. Go, Diane!

The point is to take intentional pauses so you have space to process information.

One guy who appreciates the power of pause is Oliver Walsh, founder and CEO of the creative branding agency Invisible Dynamics. "When your life requires you to be the same person playing different versions of yourself, one of the hardest things is seamless switching," he told me of juggling his various roles. "CFO to creative director to dad to husband to friend to client management to investor relations. Each requires different energy."

The key is having reset moments between roles. "I don't have perfect tricks, but awareness helps. I acknowledge 'I need to reset' and ask 'Who am I resetting into?'" he explained. "Just the active thinking about the shift helps calibrate into the next mode."

So consider how you can integrate pauses into your daily routine. To begin, set three gentle alarms on your phone to go off throughout your day as reminders to take five minutes and reconnect with your daily intention. Since my main goal is serenity, I use these moments to find calm. I labeled my alarm nudges as SOUL, HIGHER PURPOSE, and BEST SELF—and each represents a slightly different reminder to me. My husband laughs every time one goes off, but he also knows the "me" that I have harnessed as a result of my practices, which has been great for us and our family.

4. Embrace and integrate feminine energy.

Recognizing that traditional business is largely a "male construct," Sara made a conscious decision to bring feminine energy into her work.

Think of feminine and masculine energies as complementary forces that exist in all of us, regardless of gender. These aren't about biology; they're archetypal qualities that work together. We all have both energies, and finding balance between them brings harmony and wholeness.

Feminine energy is all about *being*. It's intuitive, creative, and adaptable. This energy draws things in, nurturing ideas and emotions. It's connected to empathy, compassion, and inner wisdom.

Masculine energy is all about *doing*. It's active, logical, and achievement-oriented. It pushes outward toward goals, providing structure and protection.

I very much appreciate that Sara acknowledges these different forces, because it can be so easy as a working mother, as a working woman, to get caught up in the masculine energy of "doing." Realizing the power of my feminine energy, my "being" energy, has made everything much more enjoyable and effortless for me and enabled me to step into my true power.

5. **Experience more to serve more.**
"The more you experience in life, the more you have to offer others," says Sara. That's why when faced with fear, her approach is to "come from a place of 'yes,' because you'll become more interesting, have more to share, and be more empathetic." This mindset shifts the focus from personal discomfort to the potential positive impact on others. So, when she feels overwhelmed, she deliberately "elevates up to see the bigger picture."

Finding the Courage to Be Seen

What Sara has been able to achieve (which now includes founding a hybrid sneaker-heels brand called Sneex) is a testament to the power of intentionality, self-belief, and listening to the subtle whispers of intuition, which she lists as one of her three biggest superpowers (the other two are vulnerability and empathy). I consider those same traits to be my superpowers as well. It was healing to fully own the parts that define who I am at my core—specifically, my vulnerable heart—and to reframe them in my mind as strengths instead of weaknesses. That ownership helped me connect more deeply with clients who shared some of those same sensitive qualities, such as Anne Hathaway and Selena Gomez. I suspect it's also what drives their fans' deep connection to them.

The more I leaned into my authentic inner truth, the clearer it became that fashion and style could be used to shine a gentle light on someone's vulnerability and make them feel braver, more empowered, beautiful, and full of purpose. A proud moment for me was when Anne Hathaway told *The Hollywood Reporter*: "Erin sees my idiosyncrasies as a strength. . . ."[3] I do—and it meant so much that Anne saw and embraced what I deeply believe: Idiosyncrasies are your differentiator, your superpower.

Empathy is the backbone of Selena's blockbuster Rare Beauty brand, which is grounded in the idea that we are all inherently unique, worthy, and beautiful. We are all rare. The brand's charitable arm, the Rare Impact Fund, is committed to raising $100 million for organizations increasing access to youth mental health services and education globally. Selena's openness about her own mental health struggles is another form of rare beauty—displaying that level of vulnerability is avoided in the entertainment industry. But rather than compromise her career, it has magnetized a massive fanbase that sees the real her and feels seen *by* her.

The ability to be empathetic seems massively underrated in our world. We treat it as a "nice to have" soft skill, when it's actually a form of intelligence that's directly connected to intuition. It is also a critical trait for connecting with people, which we all want and *need* to do. Laura Day reminded me of this when we discussed the importance of unity—being ourselves in tandem with others. She says: "Unity is not about everyone being the same, but rather about keeping your individuality while still being able to work with a group to transcend limitations and create something more."

Your willingness to remain open and show up with a generous, curious spirit gives others permission to do the same. It's how human connection works. One person changes the entire room—and, little by little, the world.

Chapter Summary

Threading It All Together
Magic isn't just for children—we can reclaim it as adults. Think back to when your closet was a portal to possibility, where dressing up meant transforming into anyone without hesitation. Somewhere along the way, the mirror becomes a lens for your inner critic. That ends here.

Use my CREATE method as your framework: **Clarity** (getting clear on how you want to feel), **Ritual** (grounding routines that leverage your senses), **Editing** (transforming your closet into creative fuel), **Alignment** (harmonizing your physical and energetic bodies), **Truth** (living in integrity), and **Expansion** (opening up to new style possibilities).

Working through the CREATE steps is practical magic, helping you become the supernova version of yourself.

Quick Alterations to Make

✗ **Invest in your mindset.** Follow spiritual teachers and self-help leaders who resonate. Consume content that shifts you from worry to trust.

✗ **Set specific intentions.** Write clear declarations in your journal, then boldly ask your higher power: "Give me / Send me . . . "

✗ **Create space for inspiration.** Take intentional pauses throughout your day (set three daily alarms if needed). Mini "think" vacations—walking, breathing, daydreaming—help you tap into the universe's whispers guiding your next moves.

Continue Designing Your Future

Transform your relationship with your reflection through daily mirror work until looking at yourself becomes a reunion with your inner magic. This self-acceptance fuels more confident style choices. Embrace your idiosyncrasies as superpowers, using fashion to shine light on what makes you beautifully rare.

Clarity

GET CLEAR ON WHO YOU WANT TO
BE AND HOW YOU WANT TO FEEL

"Clarity comes from

engagement, not thought."

MARIE FORLEO

If you've spent any time at all reading and listening to the great spiritual and self-growth thinkers out there—I'm talking about everyone from Louise Hay to Wayne Dyer to Oprah to Gabrielle Bernstein—you may have detected a common denominator in what they evangelize: You have to get clear on what truly makes your heart happy to attract the life success and satisfaction you're searching for—that we're *all* searching for. It's the spark that puts the whole manifestation flywheel in motion.

I know what you're dying to ask right now: "But what if I don't know what I want? Like really don't know—at all. Where do I begin?" To help answer those burning questions, I turned to author and business coach Marie Forleo, whose approach to clarity has helped millions of entrepreneurs and dreamers worldwide.

Just asking yourself "What do I want?" can feel overwhelming, especially when you've been so focused on what others expect of you that you've lost touch with your own desires. If you're feeling this way—completely disconnected from what lights you up—you're not alone, and more importantly you're not stuck. "There are practical, proven ways to reconnect with the desires that are already within you, buried under years of conditioning and 'shoulds,'" assures Marie, who says it all starts with this powerful principle: "Clarity comes from engagement, not thought."

What does that mean? Most of us spend endless hours in our heads, running through different scenarios, fantasizing about possibilities, or talking ourselves in circles. But here's the truth, says Marie: "You cannot think your way to clarity. You have to *feel* your way there through real-world action and engagement."

Consider this scenario: If you were thinking about leaving your corporate job to become a baker, you could spend months reading articles about the baking industry, listening to podcasts about entrepreneurship, and imagining what it would be like to run your own bakery. But none of that mental activity would give you the clarity that comes from, say, volunteering at a local bakery for a few weekends, feeling the flour between your fingers, experiencing the early-morning hours, and discovering whether your body feels energized or depleted by the work.

"You want to put on your curiosity hat and treat it as an experiment, as though you were a creative scientist looking for clues," advises Marie. "You have a hypothesis. Now you're going to test this hypothesis, and no matter what the outcome of that test, you are going to have more solid, grounded information to point you toward your next step."

I tell this to aspiring stylists who ask for advice on how to get going in the industry all the time. My advice is always the same: Offer to assist someone whose career you admire and who operates at a frequency that you find to be inspiring. If you have no direct line to this person, get resourceful. Send them a DM on social media or make a comment on one of their posts. Look at their Instagram bio or LinkedIn for a contact (such as a business email address or booking agent) and leave a message offering your services. It may look like a glamorous profession, but until you say *yes* to the late-night packing for shoots, the endless parade of deliveries, pickups, unboxings, and returns—and yes, the coffee runs (yours should be included in the order)—you just won't know for sure. Be helpful. Learn and listen to what your intuition tells you. If ever a new assistant complains about the standard demands of the job, it should be a sign to them that they're in the wrong place. I can tell you it's a sign to me. When you're starting out in a field with a lot to learn, you need to be in the *yes* game.

Active engagement requires a fundamental shift in how you view "failed" experiments, says Marie, who shares this example from her own past. For as long as she can remember, Marie wanted to be a dancer. In hot pursuit of that dream, years ago she responded to an open call to audition for a Missy Elliott music video. But when she got into the room, she completely froze, forgetting all the choreography. She ran out of the building in humiliation, and it felt like a devastating failure. But that "failure" gave her crucial information: She still loved dance, but the competitive professional dance world wasn't for her. That clarity (derived through engagement) led her to discover dance fitness, and she eventually became one of the world's first Nike Elite dance athletes.

I totally relate to Marie's anecdote and have my own past "failure" experience to share. I moved to New York City at seventeen with the goal of becoming an actor. I had those "bright lights, big city" dreams of being a star of the stage and screen. I quit before giving it a real chance because something inside me said it wasn't for me—and in that regard, it was a failure . . . or at least a false start. But I took something away from the "active engagement" experience of going to theater school and a few post-graduation auditions. The costuming and storytelling lit me up. While some actors spent endless hours researching their roles to get in the mindset of their character, I found that the most expedient and amusing way to get into character was to get into their clothes! And that indirectly led me to a fashion career, where I got to tell stories through clothes as an editorial fashion editor and, later, as a stylist. The bonus: Working primarily with actors allows me to witness, up close, the myriad ways my clients breathe life into their characters. And how clothes are one way they channel those characters, which I understand intimately. Seeing creativity executed this way never fails to move me.

Ready to gain clarity about what truly lights you up? I got advice from Marie on how to do just that. She suggested four core exercises to get started.

EXERCISE 1

The "Wouldn't It Be Cool If . . . ?" Practice

For those who feel completely disconnected from their desires, Marie recommends starting with this journaling exercise. It's designed to bypass your inner critic and reconnect you with the playful, imaginative part of yourself that knows what you want.

HOW IT WORKS:

1. Set aside uninterrupted time with just you and a journal.
2. Complete this sentence stem: "Wouldn't it be cool if . . . ?"
3. Write down whatever comes to mind, no matter how ridiculous.
4. Challenge yourself to complete this sentence fifty times in one sitting.

Why fifty? Because if you're disconnected from your desires, you need volume to break through. "We have to make it past our inner critic," Marie explains. "We have to go past the point of comfort to get so outrageous and so playful and so nonsensical that a connective tissue starts to form back between you and you."

Don't worry about being practical or realistic. Let yourself write things like "Wouldn't it be cool if I got paid to watch *The Real Housewives*?" or "Wouldn't it be cool if I could travel the world as a food critic?" The goal is to fire up your imagination and bust out of the conditioning that tells you what's "appropriate" to want.

BONUS CHALLENGE: Do this exercise for seven days in a row, then look for consistent threads or themes that keep appearing. These patterns and common denominators often point toward your authentic desires.

EXERCISE 2 The Reverse Engineering Method

Sometimes the fastest path to clarity is through the back door—by identifying what you definitely *don't* want.

Our brains are naturally wired to notice problems and frustrations. "We are wired through evolution to focus on what's wrong, to focus on problems, to focus on frustration because that was part of the way that we survived," says Marie. For our purposes, it's a helpful process of elimination.

HOW IT WORKS:

1. Make a comprehensive list of everything you don't want in the area you're seeking clarity about (career, relationships, lifestyle, etc.).
2. Be specific about what frustrates, drains, or pains you.
3. Take each "don't want" and flip it to its positive opposite.
4. Refine and personalize these "wants" until they feel authentic to you.

Example:

- ✗ Don't want: "A relationship where I don't feel seen, heard, and understood"
- ✗ Do want: "A relationship where I feel deeply seen, heard, and understood most of the time"
- ✗ Don't want: "A closet full of clothes that are too tight and make me uncomfortable"
- ✗ Do want: "A closet full of clothes that fit beautifully and make me feel confident and comfortable"

This exercise often reveals desires that were there all along but hidden beneath layers of frustration and resignation.

Once you've done the deeper work of reconnecting with your desires, you need a daily practice for making decisions that align with your authentic self. Marie's approach: "Feel it to find it."

This means tuning in to your body's wisdom rather than just your mind's analysis. Whether you're choosing what to wear, deciding whether to take a meeting, or considering a new opportunity, your body has information that your mind might miss. When I asked Marie how to apply this to getting dressed, here's what she suggested:

EXERCISE 3 The 'Fit Check

1. Try on the outfit.
2. Look at yourself in the mirror or sit quietly with the decision.
3. Notice: Does your face naturally smile? Do you feel energized or drained?
4. Pay attention to your posture. Are you standing taller or slumping?
5. Trust what your body is telling you.

As Marie puts it: "When I put certain things on, when I look in the mirror, my face either lights up and I'm like, 'Damn, girl,' or I watch every energy metric in me sink—there's no smile on my face, there's no energy. I feel weighed down."

I do this with clients all the time. I monitor their first reaction (facial expression, body language, energy) when they try something on and look in the mirror. That instinctive reaction is a key indicator of how something makes them feel. I not only take this initial reaction into account; it tells me almost everything I need to know.

EXERCISE 4 The Expanded vs. Contracted Test

As a variation on the 'Fit Check, try this somatic litmus test:

1. Get still and present, away from distractions.
2. Consider the decision you're facing.
3. Ask yourself: "Does [this option] make me feel expanded or contracted?"
4. Notice your body's immediate response.

EXPANDED feels like: lightness, gentle forward movement, butterflies in your belly, tingling, buoyancy—even if coupled with fear or nervousness.

CONTRACTED feels like: heavy shoulders, pulling back, pit in your stomach, fatigue, dread, or a subtle "no" movement of your chin.

This practice works because your body often knows what's right for you before your mind does. It cuts through the mental chatter and gets straight to your authentic response.

YOUR ACTION STEPS:

1. **Start with engagement:** Instead of thinking about what you want, identify one small way you can experiment with something that intrigues you this week.
2. **Try the "Wouldn't it be cool if . . . ?" exercise:** Set aside thirty minutes and aim for fifty completions in one sitting.
3. **Make your "don't want" list:** Write down everything that frustrates you in one area of your life, then flip each item to its positive opposite.
4. **Practice daily body awareness:** For one week, before making any decision—what to wear, what to eat, whether to say yes to plans—pause and notice how your body responds to each option.
5. **Use the expansion/contraction test:** The next time you face a bigger decision, get quiet and ask your body whether the option makes you feel expanded or contracted.

Remember, getting clear on what you want isn't a one-time event; it's an ongoing practice of listening to yourself with curiosity and compassion. As Marie reminds us: "Life shows you through restlessness, dissatisfaction, and loss of passion around something that a certain stage is complete." Your desires will evolve as you do, and that's exactly as it should be.

The key is developing the skills to hear your authentic voice, trust what it's telling you, and then get brave enough to follow those new breadcrumbs—through engagement, not thought.

While Marie Forleo gives us a framework for discovering our desires through action, spiritual teacher and bestselling author Gabby Bernstein offers us the energetic foundation that makes manifestation possible, illuminating why clarity is so essential to creating the life we want. And make no mistake, there is a component of action in what she extols, too.

Gabby refers to clarity as the first and most important step in the manifesting process. "When you take the time to gain laser-focused clarity on what you truly want, you ignite an unstoppable force to draw it into your reality," says Gabby. "The universe is always listening, so when you define your dreams with precision and embody that energy, you magnetize your desires."

I've read all of Gabby's books (there are eleven—so far!) and love using her *Super Attractor* card deck and "Gabby" coaching app. So when I was in the process of writing my book pitch, I knew I had to pick her brain. The problem: I didn't know her at the time. On a work trip in Switzerland, I was jet-lagged and awake at 2:00 a.m. when I opened my phone and came across a post on Gabby's Instagram account about taking "aligned action." It felt like the universe was giving me a gentle nudge. Having followed her for years, I decided to embrace that moment of inspiration and send Gabby a DM. She responded immediately. A few days later, after returning to the US, we connected by phone. She welcomed me into "this work" (of self-growth endeavors) with genuine kindness.

Before we get into Gabby's style-specific advice, below are a few of the get-clear tips she offers. They further validate the nonnegotiable elements of gaining clarity we've heard from others:

- Begin with stillness. Quiet your mind through meditation to create space for your authentic desires to emerge beyond the noise of daily life.
- Listen to the whispers of your inner voice rather than the external expectations that often cloud our true wishes. Sometimes it's

hard to separate out those two because the external voices are so dominant. You need to hold up a mic to that quieter internal voice.

X Notice what brings you joy. These moments are pointing you toward what your soul truly craves.

X Acknowledge when doubt appears (such as "I can't do that," "I can't be that," or "I can't have that") and consciously redirect your thoughts toward love and possibility. Gabby calls this "choosing again."

X Practice gratitude for what already exists in your life, creating an energetic foundation that attracts more abundance.

X Write down your desires without editing or judging them, allowing your truest self to speak through the pen—or keypad. Remember this is about tuning in to the wisdom that already resides within you.

X Visualize those desires as already manifested, connecting with the emotional essence of having already received what you seek.

X Take inspired action that feels aligned, moving forward with purpose but without forcing outcomes or having rigid expectations. Gabby suggests reciting this "prayer" on repeat: "May it be this or something better."

That last point about taking action is key—and it's a recurring theme in this book. In fact, reading this book is, in and of itself, a component of that action—the thoughts it inspires, the daily rituals it encourages, the changes it makes space for.

The objective of taking aligned action is to create coherence between your inner values and outward behaviors. It's the connective tissue between potential and actualization. So are you the kind of person who merely accumulates wisdom or one who uses it to reshape their reality? Only you can answer that, but I have a hunch you're in the latter category. So use this book as the catalyst that propels you to move beyond passive understanding into active implementation through intentional practices—like getting dressed!

Since Gabby is such a gifted spiritual and self-growth teacher—not to mention, a fashion lover—I wanted to specifically break out her thoughts about how clothes factor into a manifestation journey.

We met up at my Manhattan office. As usual, Gabby breezed in oozing creative energy, a Jennifer Meyer "manifest" necklace dangling around her neck. So on brand! She introduced herself to Carlyn, my studio director, who was visiting from LA, and Claudia, who holds down the fort in the New York office. She asked them questions, took in the scene, voiced a few observations, offered a handful of kind compliments—all very Gabby.

I asked Gabby to articulate why clothes matter. Without a second's hesitation she said, "What you wear should be a means of manifesting because it's part of the process of becoming the person you're capable of being." Boom. This is the essence of what I call life alignment through style—the practice of using your clothing choices as a daily manifestation tool and catalyst for stepping into your highest self.

Gabby relayed a period of her own spiritual development where "a new part of me wanted to emerge," she said. To summon this part, she got incredibly specific about how this new version of herself would dress: "Edgy, but tailored" is how she described the style. For example, an oversized blazer from the modern, ultrahip, quietly dramatic brand Khaite, her go-to for uniform dressing that makes her feel lit. Gabby has been loving Khaite's proportion play, such as high-waisted straight jeans, kitten heels, bodycon dresses that hug curves with elegance, luxe knits, and more. Gabby, like me, also loves brands that allow for polish, ease, and that "cool factor"—think The Frankie Shop and The Row. But Gabby's style switch up wasn't just about fashion; it was an outward expression of her internal evolution. In other words, she was dressing more intentionally. "What you wear should be a reflection of your intention about how you want to feel," says Gabby, perfectly echoing my core belief.

Given that, we need to get intentional about defining those feelings. Do you want to feel strong? Empowered? Safe? Held? Beautiful? Your clothing choices should support those intentions.

The Daily Design Method, Style Edition

One practical tool Gabby shares in her teachings is her Daily Design Method, which is an exercise where you ask yourself four simple questions that "project out what you want to create," says Gabby.[1] They are:

WHO DO I WANT TO BE TODAY?

How do I want to FEEL today?

What do I want to GIVE toDAY?

WHAT do I want to RECEIVE TODAY?

In an act of spontaneous co-creation, we decided to apply the framework of her Daily Design Method to the practice of getting dressed: Whatever intended feeling or feelings you arrive at after asking yourself those four questions should then be reflected in what you choose to wear. For example, if you want to be a powerful force in the world, you might reach for that structured blazer that makes you feel powerful and reminds you to stand a little taller. If you want to step into your most creative self, you might spring for those whimsical earrings you've been eyeing or a more boho-style jacket—think Stevie Nicks, Florence Welch, or Gracie Abrams and their artistic, free spirit vibes—or even a cargo pant or military-style coat with deep pockets for a mini notebook or sketchbook. If you want to be the best parent you can be, maybe you source some soft sets (matching shorts or joggers with an oversized top) to remind yourself that you are your kids' softest place to land. To summon mom energy, I find that changing into a housedress—my term for a flowy or decidedly girly frock—instantly does the trick because it puts me in touch with divine feminine power. My current favorites on rotation are from Doen, Ulla Johnson, and Hill House Home.

Drawing Inspiration Without Imitation

Gabby commented that she's inspired by the style of gorgeous and accomplished interior designer Kelly Wearstler, who I noted earlier dresses with intention. "She's edgy as all fuck," says Gabby. It's true—Kelly is as bold and brave with her fashion choices as she is with her statement-making interior designs. She wears a mix of vintage and new and is fearless in her combinations: feather-adorned wide-leg pants, blouses with high-peaked shoulders, draped asymmetrical blazers, knee-high boots with shorts, and sometimes just ripped jeans and a T-shirt. Kelly goes for it all, and she goes all in. She's absolutely inspiring! But inspiration isn't about copying—it's about identifying the qualities you admire and using them to make your own secret sauce by adjusting the ingredients to match your authentic self.

This is the level of clarity we're aiming for. Your highest self isn't some vague concept; it's a specific energy, a particular way of being in the world that you can see, feel, and, yes, dress for.

Gabby admits to "throwing on whatever—usually old workout clothes" when she's sitting at her desk at home writing. My response: "Don't take a vacation from your best self. She's always there." Meaning that even in your most casual moments, even when no one's there to see your style, you can choose pieces that honor and support the energy you want to embody. Upgraded casual wear can still be an expression of your highest self. Knowing how committed Gabby is to taking aligned action, she was probably on a chic activewear site adding to cart before even leaving the building.

If there isn't time or budget for buying, there are plenty of other options: Restyle your existing wardrobe by experimenting with mixing and matching what you have. Layer athletic tops under jackets or pair leggings with a men's button down and an oversized cargo or denim jacket (more proportion play!) for a fresh look. Small styling tweaks, like knotting a loose tee at the waist, tossing an oversized cable sweater or sweatshirt around your shoulders, or accessorizing with chunky earrings, can elevate basic athleisure while still being comfy. I like to look at the late Princess Diana's off-duty style for a little retro inspiration in this department: oversized earrings and sweater paired with bike shorts, thick scrunched socks, sneakers, and movie-star glasses. Because, why not?

When I moved cross-country from New York to LA, I hadn't created a method yet, but my style intuition sharpened. Choices became clear without much conscious decision-making. Some people

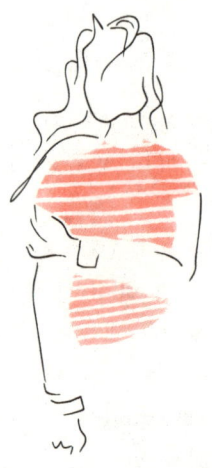

have an allergic reaction to the pollen in their new state. I seemed to develop an allergy to any clothing that wasn't white, soft, refined, and feminine—I was channeling feminine goddess vibes after years of hustling in New York City. I also changed my clothes several times a day—even though the world was shut down and we weren't seeing other people much. I needed to feel calm. My intuitive spirit knew it and just told me what to do.

Cut to five years later when we moved back to NYC, method in place—it was the exact opposite. I leaned into black, structured power pieces, like bold-shouldered jackets and oversized suiting—big proportions. Besides spearheading the three-thousand-mile move of my family of five, I had a client with a huge fashion tour the week I landed, meaning I had numerous fittings, press appearances, and looks to style, curate, create, and manage. I had to look great, feel great, and get a ton done. Needing to function under pressure has an advantage: no time to overthink. In my world, *now* is always the best time. That's the mode. And these "power pieces" help make me feel confident and in control so I can focus on the tasks at hand.

My ambitious goals and hefty to-do lists do sometimes test my patience: with others but also with myself. I can be hard on myself for not reaching the finish line of a goal fast enough. It's a familiar refrain, so you might totally relate! Even self-help and motivational guru Mel Robbins has said in *The 5 Second Rule*, "I have a hard time finding the balance between not beating myself up when it doesn't happen as fast as I'd like it to, and not wasting time while I wait for it to happen." In those moments, the act of getting dressed by leaning into my method of dressing intentionally provides a framework that brings clarity.

The systems I create around what I wear, and choosing to continually reboot and get clear on how I want to feel and what kind of woman I want to be, offer me freedom. Structure and discipline, the very method of this book, keep me rooted consistently in my bigger intention—my bigger vision—and they keep my creative flow going, if there is a lot going on around me. The key to my sanity and my success is managing to find alignment with the calm in the storm.

Over the years, I have worked with every kind of client. At times, even with people I was warned were "difficult" or "opinionated" or "demanding." I became a style whisperer to those so-called complicated women because I love people who have a point of view. Put another way, they have *clarity* about who they are, who they're not, and who they want to be. People are sometimes labeled "difficult" simply because they want to collaborate and have a say in what they wear—which is not only reasonable; it's smart!

Think of yourself as your own client. How can you best serve you? Be your best collaborator? How can you gain even more clarity around what you need today, tomorrow, and even further into the future?

It's time to start setting intentions and begin formulating a vision of who you are (or are striving to become). I don't like to think small. We aren't here to live small. Getting honest requires a bit of courage. Plus, a little discomfort is instrumental to affecting change. I advise you to start noticing when these little pings of discomfort show up. It could be your intuition nudging you toward what you need (and even want). Growth tends to accelerate when we are brave enough to get curious about where those feelings come from.

Encouraging this kind of excavation in an effort to create a cohesive and intentional style DNA is the goal of every first fitting (as we say in the styling business) I have with a client. And while your every outfit might not be cataloged by the outside world, the process I use is the same for every person I work with, famous or not. We start by getting clarity on the goal: *How do they want to feel?*

In that first meeting, clients bare themselves literally and figuratively while we explore what they want to tap into, what holds them back, what makes them feel insecure, and what they feel great wearing. It's a vulnerable position to be in, so to do what I do well, I have to be vulnerable, too. In general, I forgo the small talk. I try to listen deeply and channel empathy. I have learned how to sense someone's raw, exposed parts as well as the areas where they feel in command simply by tuning in. I block out the noise and focus on what someone is trying to tell me between the lines of what they're saying outwardly. I pick up on body language and facial cues. I can sense an energetic shift when I present something someone doesn't like but is afraid to admit it—and, conversely, when they gravitate to something I didn't even think was on the wardrobe table, so to speak. We talk about immediate goals and we talk about bigger goals. I tether myself to the intention behind what we're trying to achieve, always assessing how the choices can unite this person's inner self with their outer self.

These crucial observation skills come easily to me because I cultivate and prioritize centeredness—something I will guide you to nurture, too. It's become my superpower at work, even when a curveball is hurled at me. The curveball could be a drastic last-minute change in creative direction, an overpacked shoot schedule with a long list of deliverables, a challenging shoot location, extreme weather, or missing suitcases containing elements of the wardrobe (a stylist's nightmare!). Despite the challenges, I have a knack (and now a rep) for keeping my composure, smoothing things out, and finding a solution. Keeping calm helps me find the solution more quickly.

I remember the first shoot I was the lead stylist on. It was a big advertising campaign with a big star—one I had admired for years. On set her agent complimented me on my look, which was very '70s glam: oversized faux-fur vest, wide-leg Chloé-esque jeans, and major platform heels. I knew I needed to wear bigger proportions and a "theme" that day to scale up my energy. She noted that part of my job was to set the style bar. This may sound obvious, but it validated the importance of dressing the part. But it's more than that. I also embody the part. Of course I sometimes get nervous. Attitudes or circumstances can ruffle my feathers. I'm human. But I have learned to breathe and to re-center myself so these low-vibe feelings don't impede my performance.

When you ask yourself: "HOW DO I WANT to FEEL TODAY?" Instead of, "WHAT SHOULD I WEAR?", you BECOME NOT ONLY YOUR OWN STYLIST, BUT the author Of your own experience.

I'm like this at home, too. There are times I don't like how I look or "can't find anything to wear," which sounds absurd. Things go sideways in my closet, too! But again, I deal by relying on the CREATE method to redirect my energy and attention, and it never fails me.

When you dress from this place of clarity—when your outer expression matches your inner intention—something magical happens: You show up differently. You carry yourself differently. You give and receive differently. Your clothing becomes not just a reflection of who you are, but a catalyst for who you're becoming.

Chapter Summary

Threading It All Together

Every spiritual teacher from Louise Hay to Oprah to Gabrielle Bernstein shares one fundamental truth: You must get clear on what truly makes your heart happy to attract the life you're seeking. It's the spark that ignites the entire manifestation flywheel. If you don't know what you want, business coach Marie Forleo offers this: Feel your way there through real-world action.

Quick Alterations to Make

- ✗ **Try reverse engineering.** List everything you don't want, then flip each item to its positive opposite. This exercise can unveil desires hidden beneath frustration and resignation.
- ✗ **Practice the 'fit check.** Try on an outfit, look in the mirror, and notice: Do you feel energized or drained? Are you standing taller or slumping? Sometimes your body knows what's right before your brain does.
- ✗ **Apply the expanded vs. contracted test.** Get still and ask: "Does this option make me feel expanded or contracted?" Expanded

feels like lightness, butterflies, buoyancy. Contracted feels like heavy shoulders, pit in stomach, a subtle "no."

ⅹ **Use Gabby's Daily Design Method for dressing.** Ask yourself: "Who do I want to be today? How do I want to feel? What do I want to give? What do I want to receive?" Then dress to reflect those intended feelings.

Continue Designing Your Future

Develop the practice of gaining clarity through engagement rather than endless thinking. Experiment with what intrigues you, acting as a creative scientist who is testing hypotheses. And always remember that each "failed" experiment will give you crucial information pointing toward your next step . . . and the one after that. Go ahead and draw inspiration from others without defaulting to imitation—simply identify qualities you admire. Your personal growth will accelerate when you get curious about where *all* of these feelings originate.

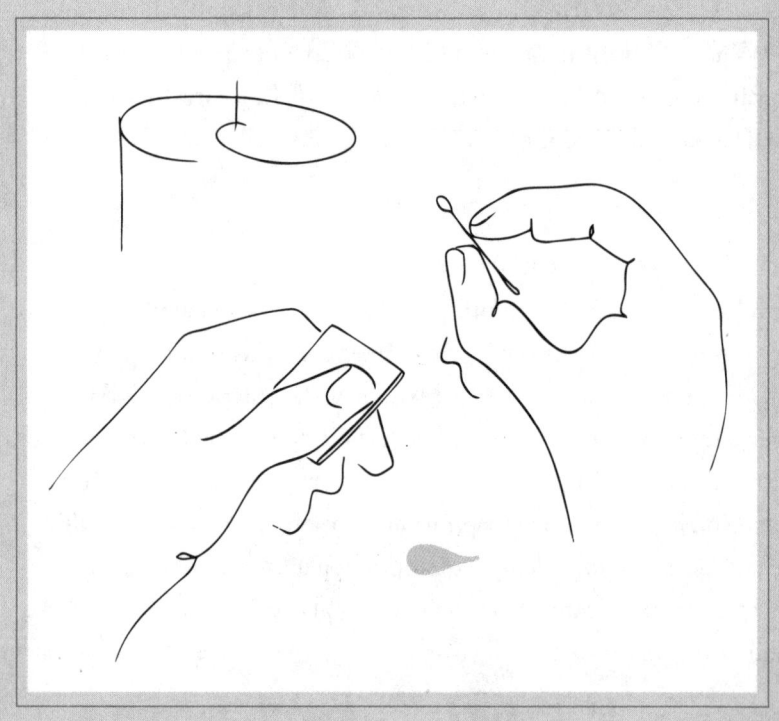

4

Ritual

TAP INTO YOUR SENSES
TO GET GROUNDED

"Stillness is where
creativity and solutions
to problems are found."

ECKHART TOLLE

I n the last chapter, I championed the idea that taking a pause is powerful. I believe this so strongly that I prefer to start fittings (when I meet with a client to try on clothes) with a moment of pause. It helps to foster an environment that feels like a creative sanctuary—a safe space to explore, intuit, experiment, and ultimately uncover what works.

So often we get dressed in a frenzy. That's true whether you're pulling on clothes for work or school drop-off, or before heading to a star-studded movie premiere. Using the CALM steps (with or without the rest of the mirror exercise) from Chapter 2 is an enormously beneficial way to settle your thoughts so you can focus your attention on how you want to feel.

Now, I want to go deeper into getting grounded by sharing some tools that pull you into the moment, which always makes you feel more centered. Mini rituals that engage your senses, such as lighting a scent, meditating, moving your body, doing a visualization exercise, praying, or just taking a few deep breaths, can assist us in getting stable even when life feels like a cyclone. Between being a wife, a mom of three, and a stylist for some of Hollywood's busiest stars, I rely on routines and rituals because there are weeks when I'm in three different time zones and I feel like I'm living in the eye of the storm.

I will share some of my personal go-to rituals, but first I want to relay what makes engaging your senses in a ritualistic way so powerful.

Grounding has an ancient and spiritual history. Originally, the term referred literally to making physical contact with the earth beneath our feet (like walking barefoot on soil, grass, or sand) to absorb the earth's natural energy (sometimes also called Earthing). But grounding has transcended its original meaning to encompass any practice aimed at centering yourself. This transformative practice anchors you firmly in the present moment, gently releasing you from mental distractions and emotional turbulence. Your awareness expands, allowing you to fully inhabit your body and surroundings with a refreshed perspective. And you can do it in a matter of minutes.

I've encountered countless moments that demanded I step into uncomfortable or unpredictable situations—whether walking on to a photo shoot, navigating a difficult fitting, or addressing a large audience. In these moments, I've learned to rely on grounding techniques that reconnect me with my purpose and inner strength.

My grounding crystal (for me it's usually rose quartz, but I have mixed it up with black tourmaline, citrine, and others, depending on my mood) has become an indispensable companion, always tucked away in my pocket or purse. When uncertainty threatens to overwhelm me, I hold it and silently repeat a mantra, typically centered on the idea of calling in calmness. Sometimes it's a riff on the Serenity Prayer (widely known through its adoption by Alcoholics Anonymous). But rather than praying to God, I ask my guides—my term for the force of energy and love that provides intuitive support—to give me the serenity to accept the things I cannot change, the courage to change the things I can, and the wisdom to know the difference. Or, more quickly, I will simply silently repeat the word *serenity* coupled with a few rounds of square (aka box) breathing: Inhale deeply through the nose for four seconds, hold the breath for four seconds, exhale through the mouth for four seconds, hold the breath again for four seconds. Another instantly calming visual tactic is calling light in—asking for peaceful light to shine through me.

I've also transferred this peace by quietly placing my crystal in the hand of talent on set or at an event who seemed nervous or in need of reassurance. We all need healing and support on some level. I try to remember this with every interaction I have. A little compassion goes a long way.

When exploring grounding rituals, it's powerful to engage more than one sense, along with other useful modalities such as movement.

If you've ever attended a Roman Catholic, Eastern Orthodox, or other high church service, then you've experienced how sense-driven elements work in concert to focus the mind. In these church services, sensory elements prepare congregants for spiritual receptivity: the spiral of frankincense smoke coming from the swinging thurible, the vibrations of organ pipes, the collective energy of people gathered together for a shared experience.

Growing up, I went to a Catholic church with my family. I was fixated by the rituals and ceremony, the reverence that was shown, and, yes, the outfits! Elements of the priests' draped robes and the habits (uniforms worn by nuns) of the sisters who taught at my grade school denoted their roles and status. Visual decoding signaled that these special church members deserved respect and consideration. The familiarity of the hymns, prayers, and mass service itself offered solace. The deep, resonant notes of the organ and choir seemed to almost shake the incense-infused air. It was really a full-body experience. Frankincense is still one of my favorite incenses to burn. I'm not sure whether that's because of its amazing aroma or due to its deeply divine roots, which you'll soon hear more about.

Regardless of whether you've ever set foot in a church or ever plan to, you can create a personal grounding ritual as a mini prep ceremony for dressing. Creating this moment, even if brief, helps us transition from the scattered energy of daily life into a more focused state. Over time, the second you create those conditions—through scent, sound, mindful movement, and more—it will signal to your being that something is about to unfold.

Scent

Scent is one of my favorite senses to play with. I'm so obsessed that I even travel with a wardrobe of scents—my little "portable peace packet," usually an essential oil such as neroli, a nontoxic fragrance (D.S. and Durga's I Don't Know What is my favorite; yes, that's the name), and always palo santo, sage, mini candles, and matches! Changing the scent and clearing the energy in a space (even on an airplane or in the car with scents that don't need to be lit!) instantly grounds me and puts me in touch with my feelings of intentionality. I burn sage around my house and light candles every evening.

To understand why scent is so powerful and alluring as a grounding influence, I talked to Michelle K. Gagnon, a talented olfactive designer, aromatherapist, and educator who travels the world to source the most incredible wildcrafted woods, resins, and essential oils for her company, Bio Alchemy Olfactive. She designs everything from customized personal fragrances to comprehensive scent experiences, where a hotel, store, or even a private homeowner will ask her to design a signature scent.

Scent is so powerful that it can anchor your memory of a particular experience or place. And it can swiftly shift your mood. That's why using scent to re-ground and reboot yourself can be an ideal first step in your daily dressing ritual.

Michelle explains that our sense of smell is primordial because it is one of the most developed senses at birth. This is why it's such a strong force of connection for newborns. When they first come into the world and their eyes are still sealed shut, they rely on their sense of smell to identify and be comforted by their mothers.

Even as adults, every breath we take is an opportunity to smell, but we aren't aware of it on that level. Michelle emphasizes tuning in to your aromatic awareness more consciously because scents can make people feel different things depending on their connection to past experiences or memories. Think of how your childhood home or backyard smelled or the fragrance the ex who broke your heart wore; it's hard to escape the associations because they are so strong.

What fascinates me about Michelle's approach is how she thinks about the interconnection of all our senses. There are heightened forms of this connection, such as with people who possess synesthesia—a perceptual phenomenon where stimulation of one sensory pathway involuntarily leads to experiences in a second, unrelated sensory pathway. For example, a synesthete may see colors when they hear music or taste flavors when they read words. With olfactory–visual synesthesia, a person experiences visual sensations—such as colors, shapes, or patterns—whenever they smell a particular smell.

But even we non-synesthetes can form our own voluntary sensory connections and fuse how our senses influence one another.

Michelle routinely asks herself things such as "What does the feeling of a fabric smell like?" One example of how the answer plays out is a fragrance she's formulating that is "inspired by the feeling of silk on the skin—it's sexy, it's yummy, it's soft," says Michelle, explaining that the fragrance includes white flowers because "silks are delicate and white flowers are often very delicate. So I think their gentle fragrance translates some of that silky feeling."

When we discussed what scents might correspond to an empowered feeling—something that clothing-wise might mean bold shoulders or more structure—Michelle pointed to aromatics that "have a bolder personality and are a little bit louder and more powerful." She mentioned jasmine sambac from India: "It's sharper. It has more pronounced edges—it's already giving you a little bit more structure there. Then there's some stronger woods that I might work with some flowers to pack a little bit more punch and stand out a little bit more."

The Color-Scent Connection
Michelle often asks people in her lab if they smell a color when experiencing certain aromatics and says, "Almost always, they say the same thing."

Red: Buddha wood from Australia

Orange: Various citruses—bitter orange, blood orange, wild orange, sweet orange

Yellow: *Helichrysum italicum*, which "smells like burnt hay and honey and like a little bit of sunshine"

Green: Vetiver distilled in copper, basil oil

Blue: Blue tansy flower, German chamomile that turns blue through distillation

Purple: Frankincense oil from Oman

I'm so entranced by this idea of pairing a fabric or silhouette and the intended feeling of wearing the clothes with a scent that evokes that feeling.

I rotate scents depending on what role I need to play, and I switch it up or pump it up during the day depending on the agenda.

When we moved to LA, my preferred scent immediately shifted to jasmine, and Michelle reminded me of the hypnotic, feminine superpower of that fragrance. Looking back at this time in my life, I was spending much more time at home and in a reflective headspace. Instinctively, I gravitated to a scent that would help me harness some divine feminine energy—jasmine is perfect for that.

With each pregnancy, I was drawn to to soft rose scents that felt gentle and motherly. For work-related power vibes, I have leaned into musks.

Michelle says that for truly important moments, she turns to a "really precious collection of oils that I use only on special occasions to plug into that energy. So it's actually more for me than it is for anybody else because nobody else will know that I'm wearing a scent derived from the rarest blue lotus flower from Sri Lanka." Exactly! It's not as much about what that scent says or means to others—that may be an ancillary effect; it's really about how that scent in concert with that outfit makes *you* feel.

Michelle suggests leveraging scent in this intentional way, which she says is analogous to wearing different fashion styles: "I can go from dressing in a super feminine way to wearing Korean streetwear the next day, which is oversized and loose. It really depends on what energy I am tapping into that day."

When we choose what we wear, how we smell, and the way we present ourselves, we're choosing what kind of energy we want to plug into. We get to choose, and we're allowed to change. As I hope you're beginning to see, energy is everything.

Universally Grounding Scents

While personal associations matter enormously, there are certain aromatics that are universally grounding, especially if they don't conjure a specific past memory:

Vetiver is a well-loved aromatic plant whose roots grow deep into the earth. That symbolism—of the roots grounding the plant—is spiritually significant.

Sandalwood is another scent that is good for centering. It has been used in meditation rituals for thousands of years because of its ability to connect mind and body. (Note: We're talking about real sandalwood, which is nuanced and subtle, not the overpowering synthetic forms you sometimes encounter in fragrances and mass-produced incenses.)

Frankincense is a glorious, ancient aromatic most often associated with high church, along with its oft-companion scent myrrh. For thousands of years, frankincense resin has been burned with the intention of imbuing the smoke with manifestations, hopes, prayers, and desires so that they can be carried to the heavens. Michelle describes frankincense oil as having "connection to the spiritual world and meditation and ritual and the way that it works to quiet the mind."

Palo santo wood: Because it's been over-harvested, stale sticks of palo santo are so ubiquitous in places such as crystal shops that burning them borders on parody. And that's a shame because, when sourced responsibly from fallen trees, as Michelle does, lighting a stick of palo santo emits a fresh-smelling, transportive aroma that is used for clearing the energy of a space, a practice known as smudging.

Sage, a delicate and familiar scent, is also used for smudging and clearing energy. Hot tip: Burning individual leaves one at a time is a more pleasant experience than lighting a huge "smudge stick" of bundled sage that threatens to set off your fire alarm.

Scent is inherently ritualistic. "It is an invitation to arrive to a moment more presently, to be more present," says Michelle. "You have to pause to inhale. And when you're consciously smelling something, intentionally smelling something, you're *in* that moment."

This connects to manifestation work as well: arriving to the present moment, pausing to consider what you really want, and, in some cases, protecting yourself from the energy you don't want to be pulled into. Just as plants use essential oils to survive and thrive—to attract pollinators and repel threats—humans have historically used aromatics in similar ways.

For protection, Michelle recommends "the ancient temple aromatics, frankincense, sandalwood, myrrh. These materials have been burned as an incense for thousands of years for cleansing, protection, and purification."

If burning something to clear the air sounds counterintuitive, hear me out: Smoke has been revered across cultures—Native American, Eastern, South American, and more—for its powerful role in clearing energy and fostering a sense of peace and spiritual connection. From a scientific standpoint, smoke can have antibacterial properties due to the presence of certain compounds released during the burning of organic materials, such as wood, herbs, or resins.

Ways to Incorporate Scent into Your Day

Scent can facilitate a deeper connection to any practice and can be used as a tool to awaken the senses and heighten intuition. In addition to using scents to ground and center yourself, you can also use them to make transitions, such as from work to relaxing at home. As Michelle explains, changing aromas changes the environment and its energy. Choose your own adventure!

Burning incense can signal a pause, a moment of peace and preparation for the day, or for ending the day.

Palm inhalation: Put a drop of essential oil on your palm, bring it up to your nose, and inhale. Closing your eyes deepens the experience because when you cut off one sense (sight), it heightens another.

Essential oil diffuser: Use it to set the mood for the day, drawing from your scent library in accordance with what feeling you want or need to harness.

I carry essential oils everywhere. Recently, I have been obsessed with neroli oil. I put a couple drops on my hands, rub my hands together, cup my hands over my nose, and gently breathe in.

Finding Your Scent Language

While there are certain scents that have universal properties—frankincense for grounding, jasmine for anxiety relief, rose for heart-opening—Michelle emphasizes that scent is deeply personal: "There are certain plants and certain distillations . . . that can offer more sort of anti-anxiety properties that can help regulate the nervous system. Frankincense is one, jasmine is one, bergamot is one. But then, depending on our own experiences, you may love frankincense. Someone else may not because they were forced to go to church when they were younger."

The key is finding what brings you peace. "It functions like intranasal medication . . . scents do affect us powerfully," Michelle says.

Creating Your Own Scent Rituals

The beauty of working with scent is that it meets you exactly where you are. You don't need an elaborate lab or rare jungle essences to begin transforming your relationship with fragrance and using it as a tool for intentional living.

Start simple: Choose one essential oil that appeals to you. Create a small ritual around it—perhaps a few drops on your palms for a morning intention, or a diffuser blend for your evening wind-down. Notice how different scents make you feel. Pay attention to the memories they evoke and the energy they create. I intentionally keep my oils and fragrances near my undergarment/lingerie drawer, so when I begin the process of getting dressed, they are incorporated first.

Your scent journey is ultimately about connecting more deeply to the present moment—and like your style evolution, it's a practice of becoming more intentionally, authentically you.

As I said, using scents is my favorite ritual modality, but it's far from my only one! Here are a few others I perform on the regular and that you can try.

Movement

I can't express strongly enough how important it is to shake out your demons every day. Movement is so important to me. Committing to some form of it daily helps me release stress, reboot my overactive brain, and expand what I believe is possible on any given day.

It's funny—I keep getting directed to movement experts, whether it's a referral from a friend or literally running into a sidewalk sign advertising a new workout studio. As a result, I've been paying closer attention to this area of my life. When we lived in LA, I was a huge fan of The Sculpt Society. I still love it and incorporate it into my movement practice mix. I became fast friends with the founder, Megan Roup; I adore her and her efficient, compassionate, and effective workout, which celebrates showing up for yourself whether that is for five minutes or for an hour, an especially great element for me and most busy women I know who need to maximize every moment.

In spring 2025, I was at an event in the French Alps for luxury sports brand Moncler. (Picture a fashion show held at Courchevel, home of Europe's most extreme and steepest airport runway, during a snowstorm.) There I met pro snowboarder Shaun White's lovely manager, Miles. He insisted that I meet his friend Hilary Hoffman, who had just opened an NYC–based fitness brand, SotoMethod. In the frenzy of moving to New York, it slipped my mind. But a few days after moving, I literally walked right into the sign on the sidewalk outside of SotoMethod advertising the studio while headed to a meeting at Gap's headquarters, which is directly across the street.

Our bodies are the ultimate TRUTH TELLERS— We just need to TUNE IN.

That was my sign. I decided to give it a try and fell in love with Hilary's results-driven method—I mean, the woman used to be a Wall Street baller, so she doesn't mess around. It's up and at 'em, so you can take the strength you build exercising into the rest of your life. Hilary is hyper-efficient and tells me she believes in "building strength one second at a time"—and she delivers. Growth happens little by little over time.

Movement isn't just exercise—it's a practice of honoring your body and cultivating the embodied awareness that becomes the foundation of authentic style.

When you move your body regularly, you're not just maintaining physical health; you're developing a deeper dialogue with yourself. This connection is what allows you to truly feel what clothing serves you, what colors resonate with your energy, and what styles authentically express who you are becoming. The more present you are in your body, the more intuitively you can practice style alchemy—that magical process of transforming the ordinary act of dressing into an expression of your inner truth.

Your needs will shift from day to day—mine do—just as your style choices do. I mix in everything from yoga to Pilates to walking to running to weights and even just gentle somatic movement.

Somatic movement, specifically, involves consciously focusing on the sensations and experiences within the body during movement, rather than on external appearances or fitness goals. It aims to enhance bodily awareness, promote relaxation, and facilitate emotional expression.

As my friend Lauren Roxburgh, a somatic educator and healer, says, "You have to work 'in' as much as you work 'out.'" I met Lauren at a spiritual retreat in New York City, and we instantly connected because we both can't help but wear our hearts on our sleeves. She is calm, kind, and noticeably present in every single exchange or conversation. Lauren spoke to the group, demonstrated the Lo Rox foam roller she created (the woman can show you how to do about a million moves on it), and talked to us about the importance of *innerstanding*—that is, understanding through our bodies and transforming emotions with movement. Somatic movement is a remedy for dissociation or numbing from your inner feelings. By reconnecting with your body you can access suppressed emotions and tap into your "somatic intelligence." Those insights can guide your decisions and actions and provide you with a more integrated sense of self.

Somatic movement can also help "exorcize" some of the emotions you might need to shed to better step into your intention, or even some of those acquired selves we examined earlier, freeing up the authentic self you need to embody today. Somatically releasing or alchemizing (as Lauren likes to put it) emotions is a proven and wonderful way to physically encourage the body to process and release stored emotional tension. Scientific and therapeutic findings show that psychological states like stress and trauma create real, lasting physical sensations in the body, such as muscle tension or discomfort, highlighting a strong connection between mental experiences and physical symptoms. So it only makes sense to release these sensations physically. Intuitive dance is one movement-based method. You just allow your body to move freely, guided by inner sensations and emotions.

Lauren taught me that fascia is essentially your body's communications superhighway and intelligent command center. The continuous network of flexible tissue wraps around every muscle, organ, and nerve in your body and acts like internal scaffolding. It's packed with nerve endings and can communicate information about movement, posture, and tension throughout your system. When you move one part of your body, the fascia transmits that information to other areas, helping coordinate movement and maintain structural integrity. It carries your stories, emotions, and intuitive knowing. As Lauren beautifully states, "The soul doesn't speak in words—it speaks through sensation, tension, intuition, and flow. The fascia is its messenger. When we listen to our bodies and move with intention, we don't just release—we remember."

Lauren suggests these somatic practices to cultivate deeper body intelligence.

The Self-Embrace: Wrap your arms around yourself and take three deep breaths. Listen for the subtle sensations that guide you toward comfort, expression, or protection.

Body Listening: Place one hand on your heart and one on your belly. Ask, "What do I need to express today?" Wait not for thoughts, but for feelings: a warming in your chest, a flutter in your gut, that full-body *yes*.

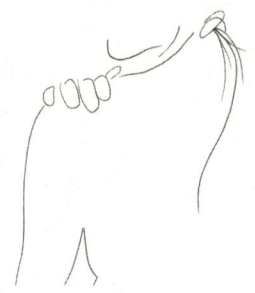

Lauren also reminded me that there is an intimate connection between how you move and how you dress—the fluidity of your gait, the openness of your posture, the free way your arms swing. She suggests doing one of these three things (or all of them, if you have time) to get "back in your body" before walking about into the world. I've been incorporating these small but mighty moves into my rituals. Give them a try:

Foam rolling to release tension, allowing the density and tightness in your fascia to "melt" away.

Stretching and breathing to open spaces, such as your diaphragm, side body, and hips, where emotions might be trapped.

Shaking out stagnation to clear any emotional residue from the previous day. Shaking the body activates large muscle groups to discharge excess adrenaline and cortisol and to break up tension in the body. Shaking also triggers the release of endorphins, which are natural mood enhancers.

In counterbalance to movement, intentional rest and stillness can be equally powerful. On days when I feel down, pessimistic, or out of line with my highest self, I lie down on a yoga mat (or just the floor or carpet). I might move gently or not much at all. I listen to what my body is asking for. It's a way to extend self-compassion and it always revives me.

Sight

Our sense of sight obviously plays a huge part in understanding what styles appeal to you, but visualization practices shore up our "inner sight" and are a powerful part of manifestation.

Visualize Your Highest Self

Your highest self is the best, most realized, authentic version of yourself, stripped of ego, fears, and past limitations. An easy visualization exercise is to imagine what this version of you looks like, what essence they embody, what they might be wearing, and what kind of environment they would inhabit. Then imagine the real-time you—with all your flaws, beauty, and honesty—meeting this higher version and asking them what you need to bridge the gap between the two selves.

Create a Visual Cue

My impossibly fashionable friend Fabiola Beracasa Beckman takes everything to the next level. Case in point: the creative way she ensures she never forgets to come back to herself. "I had been reading about memory aids from the olden times, and tying a ribbon around your finger was a way to remember important things," she told me. "So I got this little ribbon tattoo on the bottom of my pinky finger to remind myself to stay grounded in things that are truly important in my life—what I really care about and what really matters. When I feel that I'm sort of spinning out, I have this reminder on my finger to look at it."

You don't have to go as far as getting a tattoo (as cool as Fabiola's ink is). You can simply go old school with a piece of string or ribbon tied around your finger or wrist. Or you can "assign" the symbolism of being a grounding reminder to any piece of jewelry you own and want to wear daily.

I wear my grandmother's gold chain pendant every single time I travel, have a meeting that feels intimidating, or just need to channel the essence of a time that came before me. I'm attracted to the tradition of passing down heirlooms because I believe the energy of the previous owner remains imbued in a piece you inherit.

Mantra

A powerful way to seal in your grounding practice is to close it out with a mantra. Maybe you have one of your own, a go-to. If you need a little extra inspiration, you can pull a card from a spiritual deck. These card decks (easily found in bookstores or online) contain collections of illustrated cards designed for personal reflection, self-discovery, and intuitive guidance, often featuring mantras. One of my favorite card decks is Gabby Bernstein's *The Universe Has Your Back*, but there are many others to choose from. Here is how I'd suggest using this fun practice.

ꭓ **Set your intention:** Before drawing a card, hold the deck in your hands for a moment. Close your eyes and set an intention. When in doubt, start from a place of gratitude. For example: "I am grateful for this body." "I am grateful for this opportunity to reset." "I am grateful to reconnect myself with my beauty, purpose, and potential."

ꭓ **Draw with presence:** Let your intuition guide which card to select. Some people fan the cards out on a table or the carpet, others cut the deck, while some simply draw from the top. Trust your instinct and do what feels right.

ꭓ **Receive the message fully:** When you look at your card, take in not just the words but any images, colors, and the immediate feeling it evokes. Each element carries meaning.

ꭓ **Carry the energy forward:** If you can, keep the card visible throughout your day, post it on your bathroom mirror or car dashboard, or take a photo of it with your phone. Return to its message whenever you need reconnection with its wisdom.

In that simple gesture of selecting a card, you open yourself to synchronicity.

Laura Day told me that every habit in your life can become a ritual. Indeed, every action you take has the power to be transformative if you are willing to imbue that action with intention. When we take the time to get thoughtful about how we treat and consider ourselves, even small measures of alignment contribute to the broader design of our lives.

The Power of a Routine

When we set up rituals, routines, systems, and structure into our lives, we give ourselves permission to function more freely. Systems are the pathway to serenity. How so? As Sarah Jessica Parker once told me, "Preparation is the antidote to regret."

Another client of mine, multihyphenate actress, comedian, producer, and mother of three small children Mindy Kaling, has developed a rule that exemplifies the power of intentional systems: "When I buy something for myself, I need to wear it within ten days. Otherwise I have to return it," she told me. "I just won't let things sit in my closet. They have to be worn or they go back." This rule creates accountability and prevents the accumulation of purchases that don't integrate into your current life or serve in fueling the life you're trying to create. I suspect there's often an instinct or inner knowing at work behind the hesitation to wear something.

Mindy also said, "'I feel the most in control and the most happy when I plan my outfits ahead of time," either selecting outfits the night before or setting aside five pieces on Sunday for the week ahead. This is a brilliant tip for any parent who may already be feeling defeated by the thought *Who has the time—let alone moment of quiet?*" or anyone who feels taxed for time and inhibited from composing a daily outfit every morning.

There is no right, one-size-fits-all dressing ritual. Maybe your ritual isn't a daily grounding, but a weekly one, and you take on Mindy's tip after the kids are down for the night and you can be alone with your closet. Maybe you front-load your time and energy once a month into a seasonal styling session, pre-creating outfits you'll actually wear from what you have, to save time each morning.

Or maybe you curate a capsule wardrobe, making it easier to throw pieces together on the fly, because everything already goes together seamlessly.

This is what I mean by systems creating serenity: When you have clear parameters, you eliminate the mental energy spent on indecision, regret, and shopping guilt.

More welcome news: You can set yourself up for success on the road, too!

Travel Routine

Portable Peace

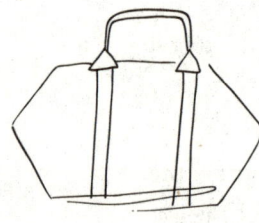 Feeling grounded and centered is entirely possible, even when you're on the go. Over the past few years, I've taken steps to make my constant work travel as luxurious, easy, and calming as possible. These routines have been salvation for my nervous system.

Packing Your Peace Kit

Your "peace kit" is a curated selection of sensory anchors that will help you re-center when you're in new environments. Pack these items in an easily accessible pouch in your carry-on. I am obsessed with having a variety of pouches within my bag for this reason.

✗ **Aromatics (scent)**
✗ *Essential oils:* Little bottles of grounding scents such as vetiver, sandalwood, or frankincense; neroli or bergamot for anchoring energy.

- *Palo santo or sage:* A small, responsibly sourced stick for clearing energy in your temporary space and matches, obviously (if allowed and safe to burn). I also like to pack incense sticks. Don't worry about bringing a holder; a halved lemon or drinking glass can be used as makeshift stands.
- *Travel-sized diffuser:* A mini, USB-powered essential diffuser, if you prefer continuous, flameless scent.

Comfort objects (touch)

- *Soft scarf or pashmina:* A comforting textile that feels good against your skin. I bring a thin, oversized scarf on every trip.
- *Smooth stone or crystal:* A small grounding object to hold. I like rose quartz to feel calm and yellow citrine for clarity. Alo Yoga has a travel tote that has the citrine crystal attached! I also love black tourmaline if I think I am going into a high-pressure situation where I might need some energetic protection.

Auditory anchors (sound)

- *Headphones:* For listening to calming music, guided meditations, or ambient nature sounds. Noise-canceling headphones are best, but any will do.
- *A "peace playlist":* Curate a playlist of sounds that instantly bring you a sense of calm. Tip: The most calming binaural beats are generally those tuned to delta (1–4 Hz), theta (4–8 Hz), and alpha (8–13 Hz) frequencies, which promote deep relaxation, stress relief, and tranquility.[1] You can search music streaming platforms for these.

Visual prompts (sight)

- *Meaningful photo:* An analog picture that evokes peace or reminds you of your intention. I keep a photo of my kids in my wallet.
- *Small notebook and pen:* For journaling or jotting down reflections.

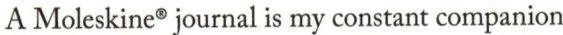

A Moleskine® journal is my constant companion.

✗ **Mindset tools (mantra)**

✗ *Spiritual deck:* A small deck of oracle or affirmation cards.

✗ *Mantras:* A few favorite mantras or affirmations written on small cards or printed out.

On-the-Go Grounding Ritual

This ritual can be adapted whether you're on a plane, in a hotel room, or on a long car ride as the passenger.

1. Scented Sanctuary (smell and touch)

Step: As soon as you settle into your seat or enter your accommodation, take out your chosen essential oil.

Practice: Put a drop or two on your palms, rub your hands together gently, and cup your hands over your nose. Inhale deeply, focusing on the aroma. If you have palo santo or sage, hold it and breathe in its natural scent (no need to light it if not appropriate). You can also rub a drop of essential oil onto your scarf or a pulse point.

Purpose: Immediately signals to your brain that you're entering a calm space, even if the environment is new or chaotic.

2. Auditory Anchor (sound)

Step: Put on your headphones.

Practice: Play your "peace playlist" or a guided meditation like Headspace. I also love Sam Harris. Close your eyes if comfortable, and let the sounds wash over you, blocking out external noise.

Purpose: Drowns out travel distractions and creates an internal audio bubble of tranquility.

3. Intentional Presence (touch and sight)

Step: Hold your soft scarf or comforting stone.

Practice: Feel its texture and its weight in your hand. Look at your meaningful photo or a mantra card. Allow your gaze to soften, taking in the visual without judgment.

Purpose: Engages touch and sight to anchor you in the present moment, connecting you to familiar sensations and intentions.

4. Embodied Clarity (movement—subtle)

Step: While seated, or standing discreetly.

Practice: Perform subtle somatic movements, even sitting in your seat. Gently roll your shoulders, stretch your neck, or slowly rotate your ankles. Place one hand on your heart and the other on your belly, feeling your breath.

Purpose: Releases any physical tension accumulated during travel and brings awareness back to your body.

5. Mantra and Intention (mantra)

Step: Either silently or quietly to yourself.

Practice: Choose a mantra or affirmation from your peace kit. Repeat it softly. For example: "I am grounded and at peace," or "Clarity guides my journey." If using a spiritual deck, draw a card and reflect on its message for the day.

Purpose: Sets a positive intention for your travel and reinforces a sense of internal control and purpose.

This routine is adaptable. Even just selecting and smelling an essential oil for a minute can shift your state. The key is consistency and intentionality—using these sensory tools to reclaim your calm and carry your peace with you, wherever you roam.

By incorporating these sensory experiences, your morning routine transforms from a hurried preparation into a powerful ritual of self-alignment, ensuring your clothing choices are a conscious reflection of your deepest intentions.

Structure doesn't limit. It LIBERATes ♡

Chapter Summary

Threading It All Together

Taking a pause is powerful. We often get dressed in a frenzy—rushing to work, school drop-off, or events. Mini rituals that engage your senses—lighting a scent, meditating, moving, or deep breathing—ground you even when life feels chaotic.

Grounding originally meant physical contact with the earth to absorb its energy. Today it's any practice that anchors you in the present moment and releases mental distractions. The best part? You can accomplish this in minutes.

Scent is one of the most powerful grounding tools because it's primordial. Movement is equally essential—it helps shake out stress, reboot your brain, and expand what you believe is possible. Somatic movement focuses on internal sensations, helping you access intuitive knowing.

Quick Alterations to Make

✗ **Create a scent ritual.** Choose one essential oil. Try palm inhalation: Drop oil on palms, rub hands together, bring to nose, inhale deeply. Rotate scents based on desired feelings—jasmine for feminine energy, musk for power, rose for gentleness.

✗ **Move your body.** Commit to daily movement—yoga, walking, stretching, or shaking out stagnation before stepping into the world.

✗ **Plan ahead.** Map out outfits the night before or set aside pieces on Sunday for the week ahead, eliminating morning indecision.

Continue Designing Your Future

Adopt sensory rituals that signal something intentional is about to unfold. Over time, creating these conditions trains your body to recognize when you're stepping into alignment. Build a scent library for different feelings and roles.

Commit to regular movement, developing deeper self-dialogue. This embodied awareness lets you feel what clothing serves you, what colors resonate, and what styles authentically express who you're becoming.

Keep your morning routine evolving from hurried preparation into powerful self-alignment, ensuring clothing choices reflect your deepest intentions.

5

Editing

TRANSFORM YOUR CLOSET INTO
CREATIVE POSSIBILITY

"Only wear clothes that
make you feel alive."

VALENTINO GARAVANI

Fashion editors and stylists make stories out of clothes. They translate a feeling into a visual language for magazine spreads, ad campaigns, red-carpet appearances, film costuming, and more. But you don't have to be a fashion pro to do this; anyone can tell stories through what they wear. I have made a living as a stylist and fashion expert for the past twenty years. When I started in the industry, red-carpet stylists weren't really a thing, which changed when super stylist Rachel Zoe catapulted to stardom with her Bravo TV show *The Rachel Zoe Project* in 2008. I learned to tell stories through fashion before I got into red-carpet styling back at *Vogue*, where I was able to watch masterful photographers such as Irving Penn, Annie Leibovitz, and Steven Klein up close. What I saw was how much intention was laced into creating those images—those stories. Every single item chosen to be a part of a photo had a role in the storytelling process: the clothes, the jewelry, the props, the setting, the tone, the model, the expression.

I find this to be powerful and provocative, especially in, say, more beauty-driven photos where there might be only one fashion element involved—say, metallic teeth on a breastfeeding Angela Lindvall by Steven Klein, diamonds on a nude model and pumps by Helmut Newton. For more over-the-top fashion stories, a photo story could be a visual mishmash of everything from fairy tales told in couture like Annie Leibovitz's take on *Alice in Wonderland* for *Vogue*. Storytelling in fashion is about using the clothes not just to communicate what you should buy, but to send a clear message or commentary on a truth about the world, a psychological reality, or even complexities in human nature. I love this because fashion is not just about looking pretty; it has a huge potential to communicate deep, complex truths about ourselves when we allow it.

In terms of photo storytelling, I like the example of the metallic teeth story; it is definitely not a "fashion" element, but it is so specific and such a clear message to intentionally choose to incorporate. The image is amazing, if you haven't seen it. The model is sitting by the pool in her backyard in a gorgeous sky-blue gown, ornate gold necklace, and gold teeth, breastfeeding her baby. Steven Klein explains it himself in *Vogue*: "There's always an aspect of contradiction. . . . So, the idea of the baby having no teeth, and the mother having gold teeth, having gold grills—it's a little . . . not a *joke*, but ironic. [But] Angela looks very powerful as she's breastfeeding. And having the gold grills . . . I guess it gives her even more power."[1]

Contradictions and dichotomies are fantastic tools in storytelling as means of not just provocation, which is a secret weapon of Mr. Klein's, but of keeping your eye interested. When things surprise you, you lean in. You want to know more. I wanted to refine and better understand my own means to tell stories. I wanted and needed to learn everything I could to develop an editor's eye, and how to tell a story with a picture image. What I would later learn was perfecting the art of telling a story with what you wear.

After being an assistant at *Vogue*, I never again worked for a magazine full time. Instead, I struck out on my own as a freelance styling assistant, and then eventually became a lead stylist. The beginning was rough. I didn't have much experience or a reputation or an agent. I remember my first meeting with a potential agent who flipped through my fledgling portfolio and laughed. "You think stripes is a theme?" I kept at it. I experimented with my aesthetic on shoots trying to unpack what resonated with me and why, using jewelry layering, color, street couture, and themes, such as leather and lace. Some results made sense, some were great, and others were pretty terrible. I soldiered on.

I trained myself by being a stylist on countless spec shoots, logging what felt like ten thousand hours. A spec shoot is a photo shoot created without a guaranteed placement or payment. They are typically designed to showcase a photographer's ideas or style. Or for a model. But sometimes they're put together by publicists or agents to craft a new image for an actor so that a movie studio, for example, can better envision that talent in a certain desired role. Spec shoots offer more creative freedom and control over how the story is told.

At first I got these styling gigs by connecting with the assistants of young photographers who were also trying to make a name for themselves. We would fund our own shoots to build our portfolios. Over time I got more brazen about directly contacting publicists, agents, editors, photo editors, and creative directors to see if they would hire me.

Somewhere along the way I started picking up jobs doing spec shoots with actors. Of course I ended up working with actors. Even though I detoured from being an actor myself, they are still my people! I always overdelivered on these shoots, creating far more looks than was required or thought possible within given budgets and time frames. I also always took special care to make sure that any soft spot or insecurity the talent felt was intuited and quietly addressed. I think that's what made the biggest difference.

I realized I adored working with actors. Taking on a creative partnership role to help craft their story felt joyful to me. It still does. Working with actors also gives me license to maintain an open heart; I pour my whole, authentic self and soul into the process. Artists understand and appreciate that.

Through my actor clients, I have also learned so much about using fashion as a tool for character development. "What you wear says *so* much about who the character is," says Kerry Washington, who ensures that choices about hair, makeup, and wardrobe are "in alignment and protecting a character as I understand them to be." She mentioned Olivia Pope, the fierce crisis expert she played on the blockbuster series *Scandal* for seven seasons. Kerry and costume designer Lyn Paolo aimed to "reinvent what a power suit looks like to have it be more feminine." They made a conscious decision to use pastels and white because, as a woman of color, Kerry could bring "a different contrast . . . exploit the fact that when I wear a white suit it sits on my brown skin differently and utilize that," she says, speaking to the deep, nuanced considerations that go into the messages that fashion carries.

Kerry finds a sense of play through characters with some roles impacting how she dresses in her real life. "What of this might I bring back into my life," she sometimes wonders. At other times, she maintains distinct separations, noting a specific jacket she owns that helps her feel close to a past character, but she cannot wear it to her current job because "that's *that* character—it's so not this person."

This strong connection to character is something I genuinely understand. My acting training at the Stella Adler Studio of Acting at NYU focused on building a performance from a deep imaginative inner life—to invent and visualize the world of the character as if it were real. I also remember being told that you need to love the characters you play, uniting with their behaviors, thoughts, dreams, and potential for growth.

This same principle of love and deep connection applies to how we approach our personal style. To get excited about getting dressed, you need to fall back in love with yourself. Open your heart. When it comes to editing the story we want to tell, this is your starting point: Get in touch with what makes you come alive.

When it comes to whose fashion prowess we look up to, whether it's someone famous or our cool friend from college, I believe we gravitate to people who rock a confidence, especially if they have the ability to make something unconventional or wild seem accessible.

My eight-year-old son, Jude, has an intuitive, zany sense of fashion like that. I am in constant awe of what he pulls off. He has fashioned pocket squares out of toilet paper, uses Scotch tape to hold down a shirt collar, and he relishes dressing up for dinners, the theater, or any outing, really, putting together matching checkered hat and blazer ensembles with a twist—like a tie-dyed Crocs sandal. His style is full of contradictions and oddities that somehow work, and everywhere he goes, people take notice. To paint a picture, a friend recently compared Jude to a young Mick Jagger.

As for my own fashion icons and inspirations, I have always been drawn to women who managed to make aspirational seem effortless—women like Jackie Kennedy Onassis, Jane Birkin, Diane von Fürstenberg, Lauren Hutton, Kate Moss, and Bianca Jagger. These are women who could be dripping in diamonds, but they have the ability to make whatever they wear seem like a natural extension of their very being—just a piece of couture "thrown on." Many of these women also had or have the ability to make a tee and jeans look elevated.

My friend Zanna Roberts Rassi talks to fashion icons on the

regular as an on-air fashion reporter. She makes a living telling the stories behind what we wear. Through some miracle, we managed to sync schedules and pull off an in-person meetup so I could interview her for the book. And honestly, every time we talk, I'm reminded of why she's such a force in fashion.

Like I did, Zanna started off in magazines. She was a beauty editor in the UK before moving to New York to take a job as fashion editor at *Marie Claire*. She then became an on-air fashion expert and commentator (with E! News and NBC's *Today* show) and she's also the co-founder of Milk Makeup, a groundbreaking clean beauty brand. All of that career mojo is in addition to her most prized role: mom to tween twin girls.

I adore Zanna for many reasons, the chief one being that she brings depth, substance, and thoughtfulness to an industry that some consider superficial. She keeps it real and has this incredible way of making fashion feel accessible and empowering, rather than intimidating. Zanna always calls me before major awards shows, such as the Golden Globes or Oscars, to ask for the details of the looks I've helped pick for clients. But she wants to know more than the brand names and who's wearing what; she wants to know the backstories behind the choices, the inspiration for original creations, and the process of how the look all came to be. That way, when she's reporting from the red carpet, she can ask "the talent" informed, insightful questions so viewers get more than a perfunctory response. She brings the at-home audience onto the carpet with her, thanks to her authenticity, intelligence, and willingness to tell the whole story. It's never just "Who are you wearing?" but more like "Why did you choose this look? How does it make you feel? What was the intention behind your choice?" She's actively curious and engaged. She is also very quick and clever.

Speaking of keeping it real, the day we met up, Zanna was running all over town, juggling her daughters' end-of-school-year festivities with work responsibilities. She came rushing in slightly breathless and disarmed, as always, of any artifice. She was wearing what she called her "comfort uniform": a baggy sweater, loose pants, and sneakers.

It was kind of the perfect setup considering that I wanted to get Zanna's grounded advice for the deeper purpose that fashion serves in all of our lives—not just for those of us who work within the fashion business. "I came up in the service style industry, helping people look and feel their best, as opposed to being like, 'Oh, darling, you haven't got the Chanel?'" Zanna says, pretending to put on airs.

Zanna never pretends about real things—like pretending to have it all figured out. For her, style is a continuum of learning through experimentation with what works best. "Most of my outfits are a variation on one theme and that's a bit tomboy, a bit girly: a big pant and a smaller top—playing with proportions."

She's created an authentic style language for herself—and from there she can iterate. "I like to put a shoulder pad on or maybe a heel. It's still a tomboy version, but those details bring me a little more inner confidence that is then projected out into the world."

When it comes to telling your story in style, you FIRST have to believe in that story yourself.

But that didn't happen the morning we met. "The way I am dressed today did not fill me with confidence and it affected the day. I sat at the back of the school hall because the other moms were all dressed up, and I was the one in the sneakers and baggy sweater," Zanna admitted with a laugh.

To be clear, this isn't about trying to keep up with the other moms; it's about recognizing the genuine impact how we dress has on our inner state. Zanna's radical honesty makes the wisdom she offers her viewers even more powerful because she's speaking from the trenches of real life.

As the co-founder of Milk Makeup, that's why she's so passionate about its slogan: "Live Your Look." Says Zanna: "It's not *how* you do your makeup, it's what you do *in* it that matters." The same goes for fashion. A look is not meant to remain on a hanger; it's meant to be brought to life through exactly that: *living*. "I put on what I need to power myself through whatever I have that day," says Zanna.

That is the foundation of what I believe: When you ask yourself "How do I want to feel today?" instead of "What should I wear?" you become not only your own stylist, but the author of your own experience.

When I decided I wanted to write a book that democratized fashion and took the intimidation out of it, I knew I had to interview the inimitable designer Michael Kors. He needs no introduction. After all, Michael has spent decades in fashion as the visionary behind his eponymous global lifestyle brand and is a longtime judge on *Project Runway*. His fundamental belief is that fashion should be accessible, joyful, and deeply personal— never exclusionary. "Fashion is supposed to make you feel like the supernova version of yourself," Michael once told me, as I shared earlier—and I never forget it.

That philosophy has guided his approach to dressing everyone from Hollywood A-listers to everyday women seeking their most confident selves. Like me, he knows that the narratives we spin about ourselves, our bodies, our style—as well as our worthiness to participate in fashion—directly shape how we show up in the world. Most importantly: You have the power to edit or rewrite that story, starting today.

When I spoke to him for the book, Michael jumped in with a message for you, delivered with passionate conviction. "Don't think that you're not in the game—you *are* in the game," he says. "Whatever you wear every day, you chose it. The question is just how engrossed in the game you want to be."

Too many women I've encountered have internalized the story that fashion is for "other people"—those with perfect bodies, unlimited budgets, or innate style sense. But Michael challenges this limiting narrative head-on, pointing out that you're already expressing yourself through clothing; now it's time to do it with *intentionality*.

Rather than starting with trends or what you think you should wear, Michael suggests an easy way to begin to unlock your style DNA: "Go into your closet and bring out three garments that whenever you wear them, you feel great. You're in a good mood. It could be anything."

When Michael conducted this simple exercise with a client who felt intimidated by fashion and needed to feel great for an awards show, she brought him sweaters and T-shirts in soft camel colors. Michael explains, "That told me she needed comfort, she needed to wear jersey, she didn't want to wear anything structured. And the soft camel color brought her to life." From this foundation, Michael created what he calls "a glamorous camel T-shirt that happens to be black tie." She loved it.

Even if most of us can't have custom garments made, Michael's example shows how, when you unearth what makes you *feel* your best, you can get creative and adapt what you wear to amplify that feeling. In his story, a glam tee and skirt were swapped in for typical event dress, resulting in a client who could show up at an event as her best self because she felt like herself. Because ultimately, the best story you have to tell is *your own*—not someone else's.

Now, it's your turn! Conduct your own closet archaeology. Pull out three pieces that make you feel like you're crushing life when you wear them. Don't overthink it; trust your instincts. Analyze what these pieces have in common, considering:

- Color palette you just love wearing.
- Fabric type and texture that feel like home on your skin.
- Silhouette and fit that celebrate your unique form.
- The elevated energy they bring to your entire being.

These commonalities can begin to inform your authentic style foundation.

Another one of Michael's empowering tips involves how you evaluate clothing: "A three-way mirror is everyone's best friend. People are going to see you coming, going, sideways." This isn't about criticizing all your angles. It's about embracing reality with confidence and making choices that truly serve you. "You can't just try something on quickly, look in the mirror, and say 'Oh it's good' just because you got into it," he says with signature candor.

This philosophy extends beyond the fitting room into a beautiful

practice of self-awareness. Michael suggests regularly looking at photos of yourself—not necessarily glamorous occasions, but everyday moments with friends and family. He says, "When you look at the pictures, you have to ask yourself, 'What made me feel my best?' Sometimes it's the color. Sometimes it's proportion."

One way you can boost your own discovery here is to create an inspiring photo audit of your recent looks, even creating a special album on your phone for just this purpose: to save looks you love and can return to for inspiration. Scroll through photos from the past few months (with kind curiosity) and identify:

✗ Outfits that make you stand taller and smile more naturally.
✗ Colors that make your skin look glowy and your eyes look sparkly.
✗ Proportions that make you feel held and confident in your body.
✗ Pieces where you can literally see comfort and joy emanating from your entire presence. It's that energetic component!

Michael also encourages women to embrace contradictions in your personal style. "I don't think many women are strictly one-dimensional, and I think the most interesting people have something contradictory about them," he says. "Just because you love to laugh doesn't mean you're silly. Just because you like to feel sexy doesn't mean you don't want to be comfortable."

This principle of balance—the yin and yang—

prevents your style from becoming costume-like or "one note" while honoring your multifaceted nature. Michael says, "If I'm going to do a collection that feels romantic with lots of ruffles, I'm probably going to counterbalance that and do a lot of it in black. Or if I'm having a feeling for big explosive florals, maybe it's more unexpected to take those florals and see them in something very sleek and clean and linear."

I recommend playing with Michael's process to see where it takes you. First, identify your primary style personality (e.g., romantic, edgy, classic, bohemian, sporty), then introduce its opposite. If you gravitate toward feminine pieces, try adding structured blazers or menswear-inspired elements that showcase your strength. If you love all-black everything, experiment with one piece in a soft color that illuminates your warmth. This creates visual intrigue and keeps your look dynamically evolving with your growth.

Michael also advocates for what he calls "guardrails" based on your lifestyle, body preferences, and comfort zones. "The guardrails are important, but they still have to have flexibility," he notes, using the example of a sweaterdress that might work with pumps for one occasion but feels fresh and modern with flat boots for another. This versatility keeps your style fresh.

When it comes to fit, Michael is the maestro. He says, "You're always better off buying something that's actually too big on you and tailoring it down rather than squeezing into something that's too small." He also addresses the psychological barriers many people have around alterations: "I know a lot of people, especially Americans, are afraid of tailors," referring to how Europeans routinely have clothes tailored because it's the absolutely best way to get the perfect fit. This applies regardless of price point. Many dry cleaners offer alteration services, so find one in your area who does. Believe us, this relationship will revolutionize your entire wardrobe. Even basic adjustments like hemming pants or taking in a waist can make inexpensive pieces look luxe. If the idea of tailoring your wardrobe overwhelms you, think seasonally about it. You can accomplish a lot of great fits if you work in a trip to the tailor four times or even just twice a year.

> FASHION is meant to make you FEEL LIKE THE SUPERNOVA VERSION of yourself.
> —MICHAEL KORS ✦

Another big tip of mine: Stop fixating on size tags. They're meaningless and vary so wildly from brand to brand anyway. Numbers don't define your worth or beauty; buy for fit that celebrates your form.

Celebrate Yourself with What You Wear

"You have to fall in love with yourself." These aren't the words of a self-help guru; they're the deeply felt philosophy of Zac Posen, a creative wunderkind who evolved into one of the most versatile fashion designers ever. His range means that he has created apparel for princesses and celebrities, designed for financial crowd favorite Brooks Brothers, reimagined what flight attendants should wear for

Delta Air Lines, and is now the chief creative officer of Gap Inc. Zac has spent over two decades understanding how clothing can reshape not just how we look, but who we become.

His own fashion journey began with radical self-experimentation. Growing up in New York City's SoHo neighborhood when it was still a garment district, he was that kid making his own clothes from fabric scraps, riding the subway in floor-length fake fur jilabas and platform shoes, and using fashion as both armor and announcement. "I understood the idea of kind of dressing for notoriety or getting attention or fame or also being confrontational," he told me when we talked for this book.

I adore chatting with Zac because he's not afraid to wield a woo-woo term now and then, as he did when he raised the topic of the "sacred geometry of your body"—an amazing and unique way to describe our physical individuality.

What Zac discovered through years of dressing himself and others is that great style is about understanding that sacred geometry of your own body and using it as a foundation for authentic expression. "It's understanding proportion and cut. It's looking at the body three-dimensionally," he explains. "It's being an interpreter of cut and volume on and off a body and the way material will move from that in proportion that elevates a kind of inner character and confidence building."

This isn't just designer-speak: When you understand how fabric falls on your frame, how certain silhouettes make you feel powerful, and which colors spark happiness in your soul, you're not just getting dressed. You're editing the narrative of who you are.

At least twice a year, Zac suggests turning your closet into a creative, playful laboratory. If you're stuck in a style stall or bored with your basics, fear not: You already have everything you need to stage a plot twist and edit the story.

Here's how:

Try the backward shirt test. Literally. "Put your shirt on backwards," Zac suggests with a laugh. His point: Sometimes the surprising style moves unlock something new about how you want to move through the world. Maybe your deep scoop or V-neck tee becomes a gorgeous open-back look once you turn it around. You can even do this with a button down, as Katie Holmes proved when she sported a blue button-down shirt worn backward to a fall 2025 menswear show in Paris. I have been messing with wearing things in odd ways since I was a kid. In the '90s I would wear skirts as tops or dresses. Even Carrie Bradshaw's "walk of shame" on *Sex and the City* became a walk of fame in my book when she wore one of Big's oversized white button downs sans pants and cinched at the waist with an Hermès belt. I rocked that look in college—how successfully is debatable. Regardless, dressing with irreverence can be so freeing.

Master the fold and tuck. Take any basic tee and experiment with different ways to fold, tuck, and manipulate it. You can find plenty of video tutorials on Instagram or YouTube, if you're not sure where to start. "Taking a T-shirt and just taking a fold and finding where that sits on your body can be something interesting to do," Zac says. Notice how even tiny adjustments change not just how you look, but how you feel. A small style adjustment, like a simple twist or half tuck, can elevate your sense of feeling *good* in what you wear.

Play with proportion like a sculptor. Zac studied Brâncuși's sculptural forms alongside Cristóbal Balenciaga's revolutionary cuts. But you don't need art history degrees—just eyes. Try pairing an oversized top with fitted bottoms, or if your top is fitted, go wider in the leg or fuller with the skirt to bring in balance. Notice how different proportions make you feel more or less powerful, playful, or grounded.

Dressing Your Future Self

Similar to me, Zac approaches styling as a form of manifestation. When working with actors, he doesn't just dress them for the moment; he dresses them for the roles they want to book next. He'll say at a fitting, "Okay, this is what you're nominated for an Oscar for. Let's think like you are actually going to get that Oscar. Who knows? But what do you really want? What's the next role that you want? And let's tease that in a way that they wouldn't know it."

This same principle applies to your everyday life. Who is the person you're becoming? What qualities do you want to embody more fully? Confidence? Creativity? Leadership? Playfulness? Your clothing choices can actually help you step into these qualities before you fully feel them.

Also like me, Zac is adamant that transformative dressing doesn't require a luxury budget. He explains, "You can use extreme fashion to self-create, which is one of the best facets of America. You can be self-created and be who you want to be." He's enthusiastic about everything from Old Navy's "pixie pants" to fake diamond rings that give you "that glass and flash and fantasy of a diamond" for twenty bucks.

Zac believes that getting dressed should be approached as a daily creative practice, as essential as sleeping or eating. "Find your own creativity every day in life in small ways," he encourages. And after decades in fashion, from dressing A-listers to designing for millions of Gap customers, Zac's ultimate wisdom circles back to something beautifully simple: "There are no rules—clothing is all just about how you hold it."

When you fall in love with yourself first, when you approach dressing as creative play rather than daily drudgery, when you use fashion as a tool for stepping into your most empowered self, that's when the story can really start to change.

And don't be so hard on yourself. I don't expect you to have it all together all the time. I certainly don't. I will never forget how I exhaled when I learned that Marie Kondo, the queen of organization and author of *The Life-Changing Magic of Tidying Up*, publicly offered herself (and her legions of fans) a little grace. In a so-relatable blog post she wrote: "Just after my older daughter was born, I felt unable to forgive myself for not being able to manage my life as I had before. But, with time, I eased up on myself; then, after I gave birth to my second daughter, I let go of my need for perfection altogether. I am busier than ever after having my third child, so I have grown to accept that I cannot tidy every day—and that is okay! When I see my three little ones playing together, it brings so much joy to me and makes me feel warm and fuzzy inside. Instead of concentrating on clutter or pressuring myself to clean right then and there, I focus on the delight I feel in those present moments, knowing we can address any messes made later on."[2]

How beautiful and freeing it is to learn to forgive ourselves, to focus on the delight right in front of us every day and let go of what needs to be released.

What I want you to commit to is the process. We all need to get used to the idea that we never get it all done before we go home, or at home. There will always be more work to do, not to mention more of the Work, meaning growing, healing, learning, evolving. When I became a mother, this idea crystallized for me. Would I stay up all night after a long day and putting kids to bed, rearranging fashion decks, and answering emails? No. I set boundaries and I try as much as possible to offer myself grace. That, too, is a process. When I was pregnant with my first daughter, I remember Moda Operandi founder and Tiffany & Co. creative director Lauren Santo Domingo told me that having children makes you learn to better manage priorities, boundaries, and balance. It all suddenly becomes crystal clear. You have no choice but to let some things go and prioritize.

So, what to do when it all never really gets done and you can't control your emotions, hormones, or feedback you get from the outside world. The aha magic? *Systems.* You came to this book because you need answers, you need compassion, but more importantly you need systems and structure to tell the story of your life on your terms.

The magic that editors and stylists can offer you is the system of organization—a means to make your closet comprehensible. We are going to learn to deconstruct and reconstruct your closet so the form (shapes, silhouettes, colors, designers) and function (energetics, vibes, feelings) work together. Your system, and your closet, will become your very own portal to transformation so that your means will be able to match up with or against your moods as you need.

Everything in Its Place

Editors merchandise. They separate by style, category, and color, and to properly view what's in your closet, everything should be facing the same way (left). That's the way *Vogue* prescribes doing it and the only way I can see a rack. But if it helps you to face them the other way, then by all means do it! Just please, for the sake of your own sanity, organize them all facing in the same direction.

Just as Marie Kondo implored her readers to look at every object and item in their home and ask themselves, "Does this spark joy?"[3]—and then to ruthlessly eliminate the things that didn't yield a yes—I believe you should look at every item in your closet and ask: "What story can I tell with this garment?" or "How many kinds of stories can I tell with it?" You need to take the time, both in the process of doing this edit and then later when you invest in new pieces, to think about how each piece makes you *feel*. Because it's not *just* about joy; it's about the myriad feelings you want to conjure with your clothes. I'll explain how.

If you've watched the award-winning show *The Bear*, you have witnessed how at the end of every shift, the cooking staff—chef included—scrub the kitchen until it is sparkling. This happens no matter how crappy the night, no matter how long the hours, no matter what else is going on outside the kitchen doors. They simply can't enter the next day—the next shift—without this level of readiness. Similarly, you need to get your closet sorted in order to dress more productively and joyfully. I use this analogy of *The Bear* because in the quest to better ourselves, you just gotta get in there, no matter how ugly it looks right now. Do it all—excavate, clean, organize. As much as possible, do it without judgment. Can I get a yes, chef!?

You need systems and structure to tell the story of your life on your terms

Intuitive Laura Day spoke about the emotional process of "clearing" items from your closet by sharing her own experience with clothes that no longer suited her. She periodically goes through her entire wardrobe, much like she goes through her entire self, to ask, "Do I need this anymore?" She told me she realized that "strapless is no longer okay for her age," finding it "not attractive." Her words, not mine! For the record, I find Laura to be incredibly alluring. I feel she could wear anything at any age. (So can you.) But this is about how *her* clothes make *her* feel. She went on to explain that this decision to remove anything strapless involved a significant "ego transition . . . engaging the fourth ego center in a grieving process."

When we're cleaning house—or even just cleaning closet—it's good to acknowledge the emotional attachment and the sense of loss. However, reports Laura, this process ultimately has led to a sense of empowerment and a re-evaluation of her style. She began wearing traditional and elegant clothes from her younger years that she said once "looked kind of sad" on her, but now, as an older woman, convey "gravitas, presence, and elegance." What a win.

Beyond shedding clothes that no longer fit her image of her current self, Laura also touched on the surprising ways we confront personal shame related to clothing and possessions. She admits to owning expensive designer bags, which are mostly "gifts from clients, but I'm ashamed because it's not within my values to advertise that." This is such an important point because it highlights how even so-called desirable items can carry a personal sense of shame if they conflict with your deeply held beliefs or intended self-presentation.

When it comes to the practical side of dealing with your closet, the method that I use to set a space for a photo shoot or fitting has elements you can use in bringing order to your own closet. I have created a very clear, methodical, and essential organizing practice on every photo shoot.

Before the client, creative team, photographer, or other advisors arrive, I make sure with my own team that the room is pristine and perfectly merchandised, meaning that the space has been arranged, styled, or staged with care so that the clothes, shoes, jewelry, and bags are presented attractively and purposefully—similar to how products are displayed in a store. Excess elements must be edited out; I can only see and envision a theme and an idea of a person once the space is cleared in an intentional way. As a stylist, I have to do this even when that "room" is the trunk of an SUV or a makeshift tent studio on the sidewalk in NYC. In my experience, you can control the chaos when you honor this process of organization.

Amanda Gibby Peters

We know our surroundings are constantly affecting us. But here's what no one tells you: Your closet doesn't just store clothing; it stores energy. The person who first opened my eyes to this was Amanda Gibby Peters, a feng shui expert, founder of Simple Shui, and a master at decoding the energetic impact of our spaces. Feng shui is an ancient Chinese practice that seeks to harmonize you with your environment by strategically arranging spaces to promote well-being and positive energy flow.

After I came across Amanda's work, I became obsessed with feng-shui-ing our home, down to making sure every flower arrangement was in a three, six, or nine grouping. The reason: In feng shui, arranging flowers this way is believed to channel the unique energies of these numbers. These particular groupings are viewed as powerful and auspicious—capable of amplifying the desired effects of tranquility, abundance, and equilibrium in the home. I applied the bagua map, a feng shui tool that divides a space into nine zones, each representing an aspect of life such as wealth, relationships, or health. By overlaying this map onto a floor plan, you can enhance areas to support your specific goals and improve energy flow.

I also started thinking about the energetic implications of applying feng shui practices to style, which was a catalyst for the formation of my method. I started exploring color and texture choices for clients through the lens of fashion feng shui. And when I posted this content on social media, I was floored by how enthusiastically it was received—intentional dressing and energetic expansion were resonating with a larger audience than I thought they would. More surprisingly, at fashion shows or awards events, actors and other entertainment industry types I didn't know but who followed me on Instagram stopped to tell me to bring more of this content forward—that it was wanted, needed, and inspiring!

I turned to Amanda to guide us through editing our closets. Her insights shed even more light on why you may feel overwhelmed by your closet. More importantly, what she has to say will help unlock possibilities you never realized existed. "Your environment is always in conversation with you," reminds Amanda. "Whether you're tuned in or not, it's communicating volumes about your energy, your potential, and your path forward. It *is* a tool of manifestation."

Amanda explains it like this: You start your day pulling things off hangers and you end your day returning clothes to that same space. It's a daily energetic exchange that's either elevating you or holding you back.

If this sounds a little esoteric or out there, it's okay. "Feng shui doesn't hinge on your endorsement—it just is," says Amanda, adding, "but I encourage you to get curious about where there are opportunities for massive improvement."

In Chapter 1 you learned that your closet accumulates clothes you aren't psyched to put on for all kinds of reasons. "What I consistently see are coping mechanisms," says Amanda, who is also the host of a brilliant podcast called *House Therapy.* "We purchase these identities. Then we stand in our closet saying, 'I have nothing to wear' because nothing matches who we actually are." Or want to become. To recap, here are a few of the causes of a stagnant closet:

- **Emotional shopping artifacts:** Purchases made during challenging moments that never felt like the real you
- **Identity experiments:** Those corporate blazers from a job that crushed your soul, or trend pieces that felt like costumes
- **Time-capsule clothes:** Items from different life phases or body sizes

keeping you anchored to the past or future instead of thriving in the present

- **Guilt hangers:** Expensive pieces you've never worn but can't release because of the financial investment
- **Should-have clothes:** Pieces you think you need for roles or occasions that don't align with your authentic self

Of course, you don't have to stay stuck in past lives or acquired selves that no longer fit. Now, the go-forward plan! Here are Amanda's suggestions:

Identify Growth Opportunities

- Spot items with tags still attached. What version of yourself were you trying to become?
- Notice which hangers gather dust. What past identity is claiming valuable real estate?
- Are there clothes that make you feel "less than" when you see them? What outdated story are they reinforcing?
- Locate pieces you love but never wear. What's blocking you from embracing this elevated version of yourself?

Create Some Space

This isn't about aggressive decluttering or minimalism for minimalism's sake. It's about conscious energy clearing that makes room for your expansion. When she's working with a client, Amanda asks: "What if we took every single thing out of here so we could completely refresh the space?" When clients feel overwhelmed by that idea, she says, "I remind them: 'That's exactly what your closet is doing to your energy every single day—overwhelming you.'" Hearing that really makes it click, right? Our closets overwhelm us on a regular basis.

This clean-slate process (pulling *everything* out before deciding what earns going back in!) gives your intuition room to breathe. When everything is crammed together, the energy becomes muddy, and you can't clearly receive the messages each piece is sending you.

- Block out uninterrupted time—several hours, most likely—when you can fully focus.
- Remove every piece from your closet.
- Deep clean the physical space—fresh start, fresh energy.
- As you handle each item, tune in to the feelings that arise.
- Trust your inner wisdom. It knows what energizes you and what depletes you.

Apply the Love Filter

Begin with what absolutely lights you up. "Start with what you genuinely love; put that back first," suggests Amanda. "Sometimes there's incredible intel we can gather from those pieces—patterns, materials, colors, or fits that reveal your authentic style DNA. This isn't just organizing. You're collecting data about your truest self."

Conduct an Honesty Assessment

"You can tell me you love something, but is there evidence that shows you haven't worn it?" asks Amanda. This isn't judgment; it's liberation. Every item occupying space in your closet that you don't wear is energy that could be redirected toward what genuinely serves your highest self. A few things to consider:

- What pieces haven't seen daylight in over a year?
- Which items do you consistently skip when getting dressed?

- What clothes make you feel like you're performing rather than being yourself?
- Which pieces represent who you think you should be rather than who you're becoming?

Dressing for Your Future Reality

A key concept in manifesting is acting "as if" something has already happened. You can use your wardrobe to embody the energy of your desired reality *before* it shows up in your external world.

Here's an example: Let's say you haven't been in a long-term relationship in a while and you're missing that companionship. And you really want to call in someone who is a business executive, like you. "Work from this premise of 'as if' this relationship exists," says Amanda. "What does that look like? How does that person dress? You might put some of those heavy-duty wood suit hangers in your closet 'as if' that guy is already sharing that space with you."

This isn't wishful thinking; it's energetic preparation. You're leaning into your worthiness to receive good things, and creating space (literally and energetically) for what you're attracting into your life. "You're programming your brain as if this reality already exists," Amanda explains. And this opens up your whole being, posturing you toward new possibilities.

The Five Elements Framework

In feng shui there's a sophisticated system for understanding the energetic properties of different colors and fabrics through five elements. Amanda helps with a simplified version of what that looks like:

Wood Energy: Growth and Innovation
- **Colors:** Fresh spring greens, chartreuse, florals, or leafy patterns
- **Materials:** Cotton, linen, twill, wood accessories

- **Styles:** Vertical lines, high-waisted pieces, cutting-edge fashion
- **Moments:** Launching creative projects, starting a healthy habit, making a career pivot, preparing for a first date
- **Energy signature:** Forward momentum, fresh vitality, creative expansion

Fire Energy: Visibility and Magnetism

- **Colors:** Reds, hot pinks, electric oranges
- **Materials:** Animal prints, leather, bold textures
- **Styles:** Statement pieces, dramatic silhouettes, attention-grabbing details
- **Moments:** Presentations, networking, when you need to command attention
- **Energy signature:** Magnetic presence, dynamic confidence

Earth Energy: Stability and Grounding

- **Colors:** Warm yellows, rich browns, soothing neutrals, sage greens
- **Materials:** Natural, comforting textures, soft knits, organic cotton
- **Styles:** Classic cuts, comfortable fits, timeless silhouettes
- **Moments:** During transitions, building foundations, creating stability
- **Energy signature:** Centered, reliable, deeply rooted

Metal Energy: Authority and Clarity

- **Colors:** Crisp whites, metallics, sophisticated grays, soft pastels
- **Materials:** Structured fabrics, tailored pieces, clean lines
- **Styles:** Sharp tailoring, minimalist designs, polished finishes
- **Moments:** Boundary-setting conversations, important meetings, negotiations, when you need to establish credibility
- **Energy signature:** Clear boundaries, refined authority, protective clarity

Water Energy: Intuition and Depth

- **Colors:** Deep blues, sophisticated black, rich inky tones (burgundy, eggplant, espresso)
- **Materials:** Flowing fabrics, silk, fluid textures
- **Styles:** Draped silhouettes, asymmetrical cuts, fluid movement
- **Moments:** Creative work, deep conversations, introspective phases or reflective seasons
- **Energy signature:** Flowing adaptability, profound wisdom

Here's the incredible truth, says Amanda: "When people start making these changes, things immediately begin shifting in their lives. Suddenly they're standing taller, their awareness expands, and they're ready to level up even more."

Feng shui is energy in motion. When you align your external environment with your internal truth, you create momentum that ripples into every area of your life.

The transformation cycle works like this:

1. You make intentional changes to your closet.
2. You start dressing more authentically.
3. You carry elevated energy into the world.
4. The world responds to this new frequency.
5. You gain confidence from these positive responses.
6. You're motivated to make even more aligned choices.

Says Amanda: "If you're trying to manifest an experience, but you're clinging to clothes that represent old versions of yourself, your past and your future are in direct competition—and right now, your past is winning." And we can't have that, now can we?! Your future self needs room to emerge and thrive—and you are the only one who can give it to her.

How to Do the Closet Edit

When it comes to the art of dressing intentionally, your closet is your sacred space of creation—the place you can craft stories, experiment with abandon, and bring your highest self forward. Here are my tips for organizing it so that it can become your portal and your playground.

Deconstruct and deep clean: Take everything out of your closet. This means *every single piece*. Deep clean the physical space to create a fresh, energetic foundation.

Eliminate the unaligned: Identify and remove items that no longer serve your highest self or current intentions. This includes emotional shopping artifacts, identity experiments, time-capsule clothes, guilt hangers, and "should have" clothes.

Intuit your intentions: As you handle each item, tune in to how it makes you feel. Ask yourself, "What story can I tell with this garment?" and "Does this align with the energy I want to embody?" Your intuition is your superpower, which is why it must inform and align with every single piece.

Take action and transform: Put back only the pieces that genuinely light you up and support your desired future self. Organize them intentionally (all facing the same direction, by category, color, etc.) to create a comprehensible arsenal that matches your moods and intentions.

A Week in the Life of an Intentional Dresser

Earlier in the book, I highlighted interior designer Kelly Wearstler as a shining example of dressing with intention. Here's a snapshot she shared on her Substack, *Wearstler World*, of how she breaks her outfit choices down, day by day. Rather than planning outfits in advance, Kelly keeps her mornings "fast and instinctual" to encourage experimentation and discovery. What's truly remarkable is how she treats each day as an opportunity for purposeful self-expression. Here's how Kelly approaches the week:

X **Mondays** are "Easy Starts" for gentle planning, so she embraces comfort and optimism in "worn-out denim" like vintage Levi's with a floral Ungaro blouse for "added summer cheer and buoyancy."

X **Tuesdays** become "Executive Decisions" days requiring a "more polished look" with subtle rebellion through "exceptional but a touch off-piste tailoring"—think Phoebe Philo–era Céline pants with a Comme des Garçons blazer featuring a plastic lapel.

X **Wednesdays** are for "New Ideas," calling for something "bold, playful, off-beat" to stay "open to new ideas"—like transforming a hair bow into a necktie or wearing an oversized bow miniskirt.

X **Thursdays** bring the "Power Push" for high-impact work, reflected in pieces like Phoebe Philo wave trousers that feel "elevated and powerful and directional, but there's a hint of casual-breeziness."

X **Fridays** embrace "Loose Ends" with creative exploration, expressed through "looseness, and a bit of eclecticism" mixing vintage, high, and low pieces that are "hard to place."

If you're up for it, weekly road mapping can save you time and also be a creative outlet. My own take on it, below, centers around—surprise!—feelings. These are some of the go-tos in my own emotional-dressing arsenal:

✗ **Mondays** require a caffeine-like boost from my wardrobe. I need to transition from my weekend self as a Brooklyn mom and wife to my Manhattan office mode. There, I'll wear a power-shoulder blazer, something high-waisted like structured denim, perhaps a statement belt, and chunky shoes to uplevel my look. Oversized suits, my favorite denim, and platforms have served me well, as well as some surprising asymmetrical takes on power pieces that I love.

✗ **Tuesdays** are for connecting the dots. I take Monday's power pieces and add fluidity so I don't feel tied down or too boxed in. This might mean a fluid short set with an oversized blazer in summer, or a vest with more fluid trousers.

✗ **Wednesdays** are for managing balls in the air. I lean into more denim, sometimes matching sets. It makes getting dressed pretty easy when you invest in set options—a fresh take so you don't have to jump straight to a suit.

✗ **Thursdays** I like to get more feminine and tap into my magical side as I try to harness all the energy I can to get things done. I gravitate toward long liquid skirts or dresses, probably paired with a proportioned piece, a blazer, or even a chunky knit. Scandinavian-style icons offer great takes on this masculine/feminine dressing; influencer Pernille Teisbaek is a good example.

✗ **Fridays** are for feeling good. "Feel Good Fridays" mean ease, luxury, and polish. Probably monochromatic, keeping some polish with key accessory elements, but I love keeping it real on Fridays with options that work for both the office and working mom life. Expect more barrel-leg pants and jeans, knits, and dresses on rotation.

Exploring Archetypes

The final step in designing your closet story is getting familiar with archetypes. In my work I explore why people are drawn to "stars." I believe we're drawn to public figures because they activate something we recognize as possible within ourselves. They show us a version of who we could become.

Exploring archetypes is helpful because it gives you a concrete system for channeling specific vibes and ways of carrying yourself. When you create personal archetypes, you're essentially building clear roles you can step into through your clothing choices.

Rather than simply copying the outfits of style icons you admire, I want you to focus on capturing the *feeling* these people embody. In this approach, we're designing archetypes based on *vibes*. This transforms your closet into a curated library of the essential ways you want to feel and show up in the world.

These archetypes aren't based on emulating historical figures or celebrities. Instead, you're creating mental and visual constructs that represent how you want to show up your life right now—today.

Identifying your *mood* archetypes helps you make a clear agreement with yourself about which role you want to step into. This process is essential because our feelings are constantly shifting. We can wake up influenced by our schedule, unexpected emotions, or other circumstances.

By getting intentional about the specific vibes or mood you want to embody, you take back control. Instead of letting random situations dictate how you present yourself, you can *actively* shift things in favor of your desired energy.

From Editing Out to Stepping In: Choosing Your Style Identity

Once you've cleared away the pieces that don't align with your authentic self—those clothes that make you feel "off," the trends that never quite fit, the items you bought for who you thought you should be rather than who you are—you create space for something far more powerful: intentional choice.

This is where the real transformation begins. Instead of defaulting to whatever's left in your closet or following the latest fashion dictates, you get to consciously decide who you want to show up as in the world. You get to choose your energy, your presence, your visual story.

Think of style archetypes as emotional blueprints—each one offering a different way to channel your inner landscape through your outer appearance. They're not rigid categories or boxes to squeeze yourself into, but rather flexible frameworks that help you dress with purpose and authenticity.

7 Style Archetypes

The following seven archetypes represent the ones I work with most often—different facets of feminine energy that we all (regardless of birth gender) carry within us to different degrees. Some will resonate more deeply than others, and that's exactly as it should be. Your goal is to identify which ones feel most aligned with who you're aspiring to be on any given day. Once you do that, you can then use fashion as a tool to embody that energy more fully.

1. **Serene:** This is my personal go-to mood because finding a bit of calm in the beautiful chaos of my various life roles (wife, mother, stylist, etc.) is a tremendous asset. When you embody Serene energy, you project an unshakable inner peace that draws others in and creates a sense of sanctuary wherever you go. This archetype is about moving through the world with quiet confidence and graceful composure, even when everything around you feels chaotic.

2. **Powerful:** We often underestimate ourselves. In fact, our "dis-ease" (discomfort, awkwardness, absence of ease or flow) with fashion can stem from feelings of insecurity and a lack of self-worth. To level up our confidence, we sometimes need to take up more space and stand our ground. Powerful energy is about claiming your rightful place in any situation and refusing to shrink or apologize for your presence.

3. **Graceful:** Granting ourselves the grace to see strength and beauty in our so-called weaknesses or flaws allows us to befriend our shadow sides (the parts we're ashamed of or embarrassed by), instead of being self-critical or punishing. Graceful energy flows with life's imperfections, finding elegance in vulnerability.

4. **Joyful:** The glorious and profound feeling of joy is rooted in gratitude and feeling whole in the present moment. Joyfulness springs from authenticity and alignment. When you dress from this archetype, you radiate an infectious lightness that celebrates life in big and small moments, and invites others to do the same.

5. **Sensual:** Sensuality and sexuality require harnessing our inner fire, confidence, and inherent desirability. To do this we have to connect with our physical bodies, fully accept and embrace them, and tap into the sensations they deliver. This archetype is about honoring your feminine magnetism and expressing it unapologetically.

6. **Bold:** When it comes to channeling a bold mood, you have to be a bit audacious with your choices. You have to move to the outer edge of your fashion comfort zone. More often than not, style bravery is rewarded, both in the compliments it inspires and in your own pride in having the guts to take a risk. The beautiful thing about that? It positively reinforces making more bold choices—not just in fashion, but in life.

7. **Boss:** Embodying your Boss energy means owning your authority, competence, and leadership presence. This archetype is about commanding respect rather than seeking approval. When you dress as the Boss, you're communicating that you belong in any room you enter, that your voice matters, and that you're ready to make decisions and take charge, without steamrolling anyone else.

I can't express this enough: By bringing order to your closet, you will bring order to your life. When you edit your closet in keeping with the person you want to be, you are editing your life to be that person. Gone are the pieces that belonged to a life that no longer fits yours. Gone are the acquired personalities that never fit to begin with. Out with the colors, cuts, trends, and vibes that don't make you shine, and in with all the pieces that light you up as from within. In the next chapter you will learn how to unite these go-to style vibes with the actual energy systems in our bodies, to operate in a dynamic, completely integrated 360-degree model of yourself as feelings powerfully unite with function.

Chapter Summary

Threading It All Together

When you dress intentionally, you're communicating truths about yourself before you even speak, so think of getting dressed as visual storytelling.

Also transformative: Acknowledging the wild idea that there is a sacred geometry to your body—decoding it is key to unlocking how your physical individuality is the foundation of your authentic style expression. When you understand how fabric falls on your frame, how certain silhouettes make you feel powerful, and which colors spark happiness in your soul, you are, in fact, one step closer to supernova you.

Quick Alterations to Make

✗ **Do some closet archaeology.** Pull three pieces that make you feel like you're crushing life. Analyze what they have in common—color palette, fabric texture, silhouette, the elevated energy they bring. These commonalities help inform your authentic style foundation.

- *✗* **Create an inspiring photo audit.** Scroll through recent photos of yourself with kind curiosity. Identify outfits where you stood taller and smiled more naturally, colors that made you glow, proportions that made you feel confident. Save these in a special phone album for future outfit inspiration.
- *✗* **Play with contradictions.** Identify your primary style personality (eg. romantic, edgy, classic, bohemian, sporty), then introduce its opposite. If you love feminine pieces, add some edge. If you wear all black, experiment with softer colors. This process creates visual intrigue and keeps your look dynamic and evolving. Use Pinterest as an inspirational catalogue of go-to styles.
- *✗* **Find someone who can alter your clothes.** (Many dry cleaners offer this service.) There is no way around it—to look and feel your best, your clothes need to fit impeccably.

When you align your wardrobe with your essence, your AUTHENTIC SELF that's yearning to emerge, getting dressed becomes the key ingredient in a larger process of self development

✗✗✗✗✗

Continue Designing Your Future

Remember that your closet doesn't just store clothing—it stores energy. It's communicating volumes about your potential, and your path forward. Once you're tuned in to that, you can consciously create a wardrobe that supports your highest self.

Applying the "love filter" prioritizes clothing and outfits that light you up—the pieces, patterns, materials, colors that represent your truest self. Be sure to regularly conduct an honesty assessment to keep you, well, honest: What hasn't seen daylight in over a year? Which items do you consistently skip? What makes you feel like you're performing rather than being yourself?

Take that a step further by dressing for your future reality and acting as if it already exists. This is energetic preparation . . . creating space (literally and energetically) for what you're attracting. You're programming your brain to recognize this reality, opening your whole being up to new possibilities.

The truth is, bringing order to your closet brings order to your life. When you edit your closet in keeping with who you want to be, you're also editing your life to become that person.

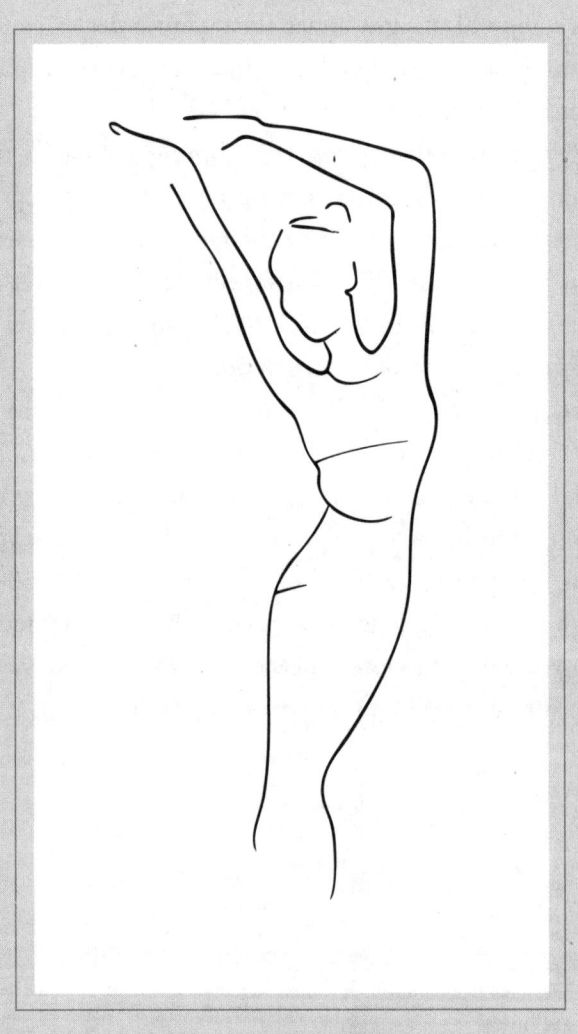

6

Alignment

HARMONIZE YOUR PHYSICAL
AND ENERGETIC BODIES

"When you are working well
with your energy, you are also
making the best expression of
your personal power....
By reading your own energy,
by becoming aware of the lens
through which you see your
world, you can change your
mind and change your life."

CAROLINE MYSS

As we get deeper into spiritual and metaphysical conversations, I want to say that it's normal to question whether manifestation or energy healing or any other seemingly esoteric concept is simply the result of us wanting to believe in a magical process, a spiritual placebo effect. (And by the way, the placebo effect is a real phenomenon where the brain and body interact to create a positive response. Nothing wrong with that.)

But I do think it's important to explain the science behind the concepts I'm presenting to give you the full picture. At the end of the day, this book is an offering—something for you to take in, digest, contemplate, and then use in whatever ways work for you. What matters most to me is that you believe in the infinite possibilities you already possess, with the understanding that igniting all that interior power does often take an outside source. Consider how the chlorophyll in a plant's leaves contains the capability to convert carbon dioxide and water into sugar that nourishes the plant, but this process is only triggered when sunlight (an external energy source) strikes the leaf. Fashion is like that. It's the igniter—the nourishment for manifesting your life desires.

Manifestation is all about aligning what you desire with how you feel. Dr. Tara Swart is a world-renowned neuroscientist, psychiatrist, and bestselling author who connects neuroscience with ancient wisdom and spirituality, making principles such as manifestation easier to understand (and believe!) by explaining the neurological mechanisms underlying these practices. For example, Dr. Swart gives us concrete evidence for practices that might otherwise seem mystical, revealing research that proves visualization literally strengthens neural pathways, that group chanting synchronizes brain waves, and that spending time in nature measurably improves brain function.

For me, scientific facts don't take away from the wonder of spiritual practices; they just give my analytical mind permission to engage with them more freely. Science is opening the door a bit wider, allowing more people to access the power of manifestation, personal growth, and healing. And that's a good thing.

I also find it validating that some of these practices have persisted across cultures for millennia (hence the term *ancient wisdom*). Before there were scientific tools to measure things in a lab there were only lore, faith, and personal experience to go on. (Just as for centuries fashion has been a means to convey status, provenance, religious beliefs, and more—what you wear has always affected how you are seen.)

New research affords us new findings. Now, nearly everything is traceable or researchable, and our minds are always seeking an explanation, especially for things that seem to have no explanation. And though I'm comfortable with the mystery of how manifestation works, I also find the neuroscience really validating to what I already intuited to be true. So I tracked down Dr. Swart to ask her some questions about the intersection of neuroscience and manifestation.

The first thing I wanted to ask her was how manifestation changes the brain. She explained that neuroplasticity—the brain's ability to form new neural connections, to change and adapt in response to learning or life experiences—is the brain's superpower when it comes to changing your mental-emotional health and your life as a whole. "Manifesting is not as simple as erasing existing negative thought patterns (*'I'll never be that/have that'*)," says Dr. Swart. "We must create and strengthen *new* neural pathways through deliberate, consistent practice until these new patterns become the dominant ones."

This biological process of neuroplasticity requires time and persistence—a principle long recognized in spiritual traditions. Our ancestors weren't as interested in shortcuts and instant gratification as we are. It just wasn't an option or an expectation. As for us in today's instant-access culture, we have to unlearn our impatience and rebuild our muscle of tolerance to wait and work for good things.

Dr. Swart went on to say that to manifest successfully, you need to get in alignment with your true wishes through "magnetic desire," which she describes as "the alignment of one's head, heart, and gut to pursue authentic aspirations." From a neuroscientific perspective, this involves integrating multiple brain systems: the logical cognitive functions (head), the emotional limbic system (heart), and the intuitive nervous system (gut). "When a desire engages all of these systems, it creates a coherent, powerful directive for the brain that enhances the likelihood of manifestation," explains Dr. Swart. "Manifestation isn't passive. Focusing on our desires, visualizing them becoming true, and directing our energy towards them through our actions—that's how it works."

Action with visualization. Dr. Swart prefers the term *action boards* to *vision boards* because "visualization alone isn't enough—taking tangible steps toward our goals strengthens the neural pathways associated with achieving those goals," she explains.

This is why learning and using the CREATE method won't shift anything in a meaningful way if you only implement it once.

Habits, rituals, and systems make a difference in our lives through consistency. Manifestation is a by-product of consistent practices.

Anyone who has ever tried to stick to a workout regimen knows that consistency can be elusive. And change (even positive change) can feel a bit risky. Dr. Swart has insight into how this makes manifestation challenging. Dr. Swart explains that our brains are programmed with a strong bias toward risk avoidance. They are approximately two and a half times more oriented toward avoiding potential threats than seeking rewards. There is a time-tested fix: Ancient wisdom traditions that encourage abundant thinking help counteract this biological tendency by shifting your brain chemistry so that it pumps out fewer stress hormones (like cortisol, which triggers the negative "fight or flight" response) in favor of beneficial compounds (like oxytocin, which is associated with trust, connection, and positive emotional states). "This neurochemical shift creates more favorable conditions for pursuing goals and taking calculated risks," says Dr. Swart.

In other words, when you intentionally engage the superpower of your own brain's neuroplasticity, you begin to believe in new possibilities for the change you seek. And when you believe such meaningful change is possible, you are empowered to take more risks, creating momentum in the direction of your desires.

Many ancient practices such as group chanting, drumming, and singing have now been scientifically validated in terms of their value to cultivating a community of care. Tara Swart's research shows that these activities, far beyond a shared pastime, can create "entrainment"—a synchronization of heart rates and brain waves among participants that fosters cooperation and promotes the release of oxytocin, a neurochemical often called the "bonding hormone" because it supports trust, social connection, and emotional closeness. Similarly, spending time in nature and engaging in creative activities enhances connectivity between different regions of the brain, improving cognitive flexibility, emotional regulation, and problem-solving abilities. These findings explain why certain ancient spiritual practices have been consistently valued across diverse cultures—in some cases, for thousands of years.

Dr. Swart says that advances in neuroscience, particularly brain scanning technology, "have given credence to things that I had intuitively felt but as a scientist, hesitated to trust—as well as affirming the ancient wisdom from my Indian heritage."

In her newest book, *The Signs: The New Science of How to Trust Your Instincts*, Dr. Swart goes even further, exploring topics such as near-death experiences and terminal lucidity that delve into how consciousness may extend beyond the physical limitations of the brain.

It never ceases to amaze me how much we've unlearned through the ages and how resistant we can be to the knowledge of ancient wisdom—that is, until modern science comes and proves it out.

Though the wisdom I refer to in this chapter is ancient, it may be brand new to you. So let me get into the details. One of the most important and widely respected systems of the body is the chakra system, which I briefly touched on in Chapter 1 when I was describing how the seven energy centers that make up the system run vertically through your body and represent gateways where your emotional, spiritual, and physical sides coexist. The chakra system is integral to many practices, including: yoga, which focuses on balancing the chakras through postures (asanas), breath control (pranayama), and meditation; energy healing, which works with chakras to heal and balance the body's flow of energy; and Ayurveda, the traditional Indian system of medicine, which aims to achieve harmony and balance within the body, mind, and spirit by aligning and activating the chakras.

It might also be interesting for you to know that the chakra system from Indian yogic tradition and traditional Chinese medicine (TCM) take remarkably parallel approaches to understanding the body's energetic nature. It seems major to me that two separate ancient cultures developed strikingly similar frameworks for viewing human energy systems.

Both traditions recognize the body as containing subtle energetic pathways that directly influence physical health, emotional balance, and overall well-being. The Indian system identifies seven primary energy centers (chakras) positioned along the spine, while TCM maps an intricate network of meridians through which qi flows throughout the body. And, the chakra locations correspond with significant meridian junction points.

This aspect of human existence is often referred to as "the subtle body"—yet integral to health and vitality—a multilayered system of energetic fields, channels, and centers that interact with the physical body.

Style and Your Chakras

No doubt you've heard and read a lot of fashion advice over the years that focused on silhouettes (aka shapes), proportion (how different shapes and weights play off each other), and color (how certain hues impact you and others). That advice may have been perfectly valid, but real style power comes from understanding how to take those more pragmatic or concrete aspects of fashion and align them with the inherent qualities and powers of your energy centers.

In the next chapter, we'll delve into living your truth, or living in integrity. But there is also the integrity of your physical form to consider, where you harmonize your body's natural systems and energy centers to better support your goals. You want these systems to share in intention. How you dress should work in concert with these systems—be in flow with them. To put it simply, when you learn to use fashion to harness your body's energies, chakras, and natural systems, you better learn to be in harmony with yourself—past, present, and future.

Isn't it wild to think you can turn up the volume on your essence when you align your fashion choices with not only your physical body but your energetic body, too?

Building on our understanding of the chakras, let's take a look at how different silhouettes and colors can interact with each of your seven energy centers, moving from the root to the crown.

Here's a guided look at the seven main chakras:

1. ROOT CHAKRA: STABILITY AND GROUNDING

Location: Base of the spine

Focus: Security, stability, basic needs, and feelings of groundedness

Style Takeaway: Structured, foundational, and sturdy pieces that provide a sense of strong connection to the earth. If the idea is to feel grounded, you literally need to feel solid, not shaky. A boot with lug sole, a heavier-texture jacket, or a sturdy jean, like barrel leg, can help you feel held.

Key Silhouettes and Examples:

- ✗ Tailored trousers and barrel-leg jeans that make you hold your posture a bit more rigidly and upright
- ✗ A-line skirts that provide stable structure
- ✗ Structured blazers with strong lines
- ✗ Supportive undergarments that create a solid foundation
- ✗ Chunky boots—think lug soles or sturdy block heels—that connect you to the ground
- ✗ Military jackets, utility pants, cargo chore coats or pants with weight and substance

2. SACRAL CHAKRA: CREATIVITY AND FLOW

Location: Lower abdomen, below the navel

Focus: Emotion, sensuality, creativity, pleasure, and sexuality

Style Takeaway: Fluid, comfortable pieces that allow for natural movement and celebrate the body's curves without constriction. Think of the sensual elements in nature—like a lily: expressive, delicate, and graceful.

Key Silhouettes and Examples:

- ✗ Flowing dresses that move with your body
- ✗ Wide-leg pants that allow unrestricted movement
- ✗ Soft knitwear that drapes beautifully
- ✗ Wrap styles that embrace natural curves
- ✗ Anything that embodies divine feminine energy and goddess-like fluidity

3. SOLAR PLEXUS CHAKRA: POWER AND CONFIDENCE

Location: Upper abdomen, stomach area

Focus: Personal power, self-esteem, willpower, and confidence

Style Takeaway: Confident, defined, and empowering styles that emphasize the waist or create strong, assertive lines. The power suit is the ultimate example.

Key Silhouettes and Examples:

- ✗ Belted dresses and blazers that define the waist
- ✗ Tailored jumpsuits that show strength
- ✗ Strong shoulder lines and shoulder pads (a secret weapon for any garment)
- ✗ Fitted silhouettes that highlight your core
- ✗ '70s-style trousers that demand platform heels—structure meets power

4. HEART CHAKRA: LOVE AND COMPASSION

Location: Center of the chest

Focus: Love, compassion, connection, and emotional balance

Style Takeaway: Open, soft, and inviting styles that draw attention to the chest area with gentle necklines. Think of pieces that suggest openness and welcome. More severe cuts and shapes might read as confrontational, whereas a silky shirt, soft knit, or rounded neckline suggests a more openhearted, generous vibe. Many bohemian styles offer this, and when we all needed some more love during the pandemic, loungey knit sets boomed in popularity. It wasn't just comfort; we needed a bit more heart.

Key Silhouettes and Examples:

✗ Open necklines and soft V-necks
✗ Layered necklaces that draw attention to the heart center
✗ Voluminous sleeves that create a sense of embrace
✗ Feminine dresses—eyelet or with ruffled skirts
✗ Soft, open cashmere pieces that suggest approachability

5. THROAT CHAKRA: EXPRESSION AND TRUTH

Location: Throat

Focus: Communication, self-expression, speaking your truth

Style Takeaway: Styles that frame or highlight the neck and shoulders, encouraging clear expression. Think of the power collar; there's a reason royalty like Queen Elizabeth I demanded this style.

Key Silhouettes and Examples:
- ✗ High necklines that frame the throat
- ✗ Statement collars that command attention, or even the classics: a romantic Victorian collar or more structured tuxedo collar (which I *love* on a woman)
- ✗ Scarves that draw focus to the neck area
- ✗ Sleeveless tops or dresses that emphasize the shoulder line
- ✗ Asymmetrical necklines that draw attention upward

6. THIRD EYE CHAKRA: INTUITION AND WISDOM

Location: Forehead, between the eyebrows

Focus: Intuition, insight, inner wisdom, and imagination

Style Takeaway: Evocative, subtle, and slightly mysterious pieces that suggest depth and introspection without being overly flashy. Think magical, mysterious, unknowable—full of possibility.

Key Silhouettes and Examples:
- ✗ Flowing capes that suggest depth
- ✗ Minimalist designs with intriguing details such as bold gold hardware, a fur fringe, or a well-placed pleat line
- ✗ Ethereal fabrics that hint at otherworldliness—think items that offer a bit of a "wizard" vibe. Don't knock the wizard adage. In so many ways little "magical" elements in our wardrobe can help us tap into our inner magic. A lot of Khaite flimsy dresses and blouses I wear do this for me quite often, especially when I want

to harness and project a certain confidence that also has a bit of mystery.

7. CROWN CHAKRA: SPIRITUALITY AND CONNECTION

Location: Top of the head

Focus: Spiritual connection, enlightenment, higher consciousness, and universal awareness

Style Takeaway: Light, expansive, and transcendent styles that feel boundless and airy, suggesting connection to something greater than yourself.

Key Silhouettes and Examples:

✗ Maxi dresses that flow endlessly

✗ Full-length caftans

✗ Sheer fabrics like chiffon or organza that seem to defy gravity

✗ Garments with gentle volume such as wide-leg palazzos or tiered ruffle dresses that create an ethereal presence

✗ Balloon sleeves or poet sleeves, which you can tuck into a high-waisted skirt or pant for a romantic look

✗ You could even play up your crown with a headband, silk scarf hair tie, or updo to elevate your presence.

Laura Day

I was working on this chapter while on a train to Newport, Rhode Island, for a customer brand event this summer, and I vividly recall looking out the window and seeing a rainbow while thinking of this chakra map and figuring out how to describe how our energy possibility can align with the way we incorporate fashion into our lives. Besides Dr. Swart's work, one of my touchstones that I offer to grieving friends has been renowned psychic medium Laura Lynne Jackson's book *Signs: The Secret Language of the Universe*. It shows you how to engage with your guides and recognize and call in signs from past loved ones to communicate with those we have lost. The journey to writing this book began many years ago, when I was a young girl at my grandmother Jane's house, a house away from our house growing up. As a young girl and through high school, I would go there to hang with her, get quality time, play the piano, catch up on *W* magazines in her armchair next to the piano, read books on Jackie Onassis and the Kennedys, listen to Nat King Cole songs, and watch Audrey Hepburn films. In harnessing the tools of Laura Lynne Jackson's book, for years I have known that my sign for her is the rainbow. Rainbows are the universal symbol for magic, possibility, transformation, and potential. I sing "Somewhere Over the Rainbow" to my children as they fall asleep—the same song my aunts sang to my grandmother as she lay dying. I sing it to the kids at bedtime to keep her in the picture, alive in our hearts. It feels very fitting that in the writing of this method I would be reminded with a sign of the person who led me here from the beginning.

As we learn about the chakras, world-renowned intuitive Laura Day is once again an excellent guide. Laura calls the chakras our seven "ego centers," and by engaging them, we can channel that rainbow in our everyday. Since Laura describes the chakras as ego centers, I also want to offer you a chakra rainbow with her ego center input. By consciously choosing silhouettes that resonate with the energetic qualities you wish to cultivate, you transform getting dressed into a powerful act of self-alignment. We can learn to harness this when exploring style direction. As a stylist, I sometimes choose colors based on how they will activate or balance these centers and the energetic vibe they will emit.

Once you know the color map of the chakras, you, too, can step into your intentional energy for the day, no matter what it holds. I should note that just because there is a color associated with a chakra, that does not mean this is the color you need to wear, as we explored in feng shui when we edited our closet in Chapter 5. The colors of the chakras align more with the *feeling* of each energy center. First, let's create a system to harness your energy for the day.

The Daily Practice for Energy Alignment

As you stand before your closet, take a breath and connect with your intention for the day. Move through the seven centers as feels natural, trusting that this practice will become more intuitive and fluid over time.

Remember there's no perfect way to do this—only your way. Some mornings you might focus on just one or two centers. Other days, you might naturally flow through all seven. Trust your inner wisdom and allow this practice to evolve with you.

Your clothing is a language, and you are the author of its message. Here is how Laura describes working with your seven ego centers as you get dressed each day.

First Ego Center / Root Chakra: Grounding Your Presence

Color: Red, symbolizing grounding, security, and survival

Begin by asking yourself: **"Does this make me feel solid, grounded, and authentically part of the world I'm entering today?"**

This center celebrates your need for stability, security, and genuine connection. Whether it's the weight of a favorite sweater that feels like an embrace or shoes that connect you confidently to the earth beneath your feet, honor what makes you feel genuinely at home in your body and your world.

Your grounding choices don't have to be obvious; they simply need to resonate with your deep sense of safety and belonging. For example, maybe it's not the glove boots that make you feel like you can stand on solid ground, but the heirloom locket your great-grandmother once wore. Trust what makes you feel both comfortable and capable of showing up fully.

Second Center / Sacral Chakra: Expression and Sacred Bounaries

Color: Orange, associated with creativity, emotions, and pleasure

Consider this question: **"Does this create both beautiful expression and healthy boundaries for me?"**

Your clothing can simultaneously celebrate your creativity while establishing the protective space you need to feel nourished and joyful. Even something as simple as perfectly pressed pajamas can honor this center—expressing care for yourself while creating boundaries that support your rest and renewal. This is about dressing in ways that feed your soul while protecting your precious energy.

Third Center / Solar Plexus Chakra: Empowered Action

Color: Yellow, representing personal power, confidence, and self-esteem

Ask yourself: **"Can I move freely and accomplish everything I dream of doing while wearing this?"**

Your clothing should never limit your ability to reach for the stars—literally or metaphorically. Whether you're stretching toward high shelves, embracing loved ones, or pivoting toward unexpected opportunities, your attire should support every movement with grace and ease.

This isn't just about physical comfort. When your clothing moves with you rather than against you, you're free to pursue any direction you desire.

Fourth Center / Heart Chakra: Values in Beautiful Form

Color: Green, symbolizing love, compassion, and emotional healing

Reflect deeply: **"Does what I'm wearing truly express my values and make me feel genuinely beautiful?"**

This center invites you to dress from your heart, choosing pieces that reflect not just what looks good, but what feels aligned with your deepest truths. Perhaps this means selecting items that weren't made through exploitation or choosing to showcase craftsmanship over price tags. Maybe it's wearing that silk blouse that makes you feel radiant, or choosing colors that celebrate your natural beauty.

Fifth Center / Throat Chakra: Your Voice in Vivid Color

Color: Blue, linked to communication, self-expression, and truth

Consider this: **"How does this outfit help me express my unique voice and invite the connections I desire?"**

This center recognizes you as the natural leader you are, inviting you to dress in ways that spark meaningful conversations and connections. Your clothing becomes a visual invitation to the world, communicating your openness to collaboration, your unique perspective, and your readiness to contribute something valuable to every interaction.

Think about how different outfits might invite different responses. You're not trying to fit in; you're courageously standing out in ways that attract your kindred and amplify your natural influence. Those shoes you love but aren't sure you can pull off? You can. That red lip you've been loving but have been too afraid to try? It's time. If you are the only one holding yourself back from style choices that feel risky, consider this your permission slip to go all in on the direction of your desires.

Sixth Center / Third Eye Chakra: Intuitive Intelligence

Color: Indigo, representing intuition, insight, and spiritual awareness

Ask yourself this question: **"What does my intuition know about this day that my logical mind hasn't yet considered?"**

This center honors both your analytical mind and your intuitive genius, inviting you to dress with practical wisdom and intuitive foresight. Maybe you grab a jacket even though the forecast looks clear, trusting the subtle feeling that you might need it. Perhaps you choose an outfit that positions you to be taken seriously in an important conversation, or select accessories that make you feel particularly confident for challenges you sense ahead. This can be especially useful when you're showing up to an event or gathering and you're not sure what the dress code will be. Let your intuition guide you.

This is about trusting the deeper intelligence that comes from the integration of your rational mind and your intuitive knowing.

Seventh Center / Crown Chakra: Unity and Transcendent Style

Color: Violet (or white), associated with higher consciousness, spiritual connection, and enlightenment

Contemplate this: **"How does my choice in clothing help me connect authentically with others while honoring my individual truth?"**

This highest center celebrates the balance between maintaining your unique essence and creating unity with the groups and experiences you value. It's about using your personal style as a bridge—honoring your individuality while showing respect and consideration for others and the situations you enter.

Laura relayed an example from her own lived experience. "When my husband's out of town, I host sleepover parties with my girlfriends, and I get us all matching pajamas," says Laura, who began to see these occasions as a fascinating expression in unity versus individuality. "Everyone has different bodies, different color palettes, different sensory needs. I need to sleep in silk, cotton, or cashmere depending on the season—never anything artificial. But it's funny how we've all settled into wanting a different kind of loveliness. But true unity isn't sameness. Unity might mean giving up the identical nightgown idea and going with the same color palette instead. Or maybe giving up both and just committing to the same vibe. Real unity is keeping your individuality while still being able to work with the group to create something larger than yourself."

The Inside Way and the Outside Way

As you explore each ego or energy center, remember that you can approach your choices from both an "inside way" (honoring how clothing makes you feel internally) and an "outside way" (considering the energy and response you want to create in the world). Both approaches work together. Your clothing speaks a language that others read and respond to, and their responses become part of your experience—an intentional energy exchange.

Game to go deeper? You can layer on sacred geometry, which refers to a body of knowledge and symbolism centered on specific geometric shapes, patterns, and proportions that are believed to hold spiritual, mystical, or cosmological significance. These forms are often considered "sacred" because they reflect the underlying order and harmony of nature and the universe.

When I spoke with fashion designer Zac Posen about his use of proportion, symmetry, and "body mapping," he brought up the idea of using sacred geometry, and harnessing the divine canvas of our body to manifest a higher beauty within ourselves to the world. To tie it all together—chakras, ego centers, and your own sacred geometry—let's break it down. Sacred geometry can work as a guide to choose which proportions and wardrobe pieces best serve your body and your chakras.

Sacred Geometry and Your Wardrobe

Sacred geometry explores the fundamental patterns of creation found throughout nature and the universe. When applied to your personal style, it offers a profound way to connect with the inherent harmony and balance within your own body. This isn't about rigid rules, but about understanding the energetic flow and aesthetic resonance that certain shapes and proportions evoke. Have you wondered sometimes why certain silhouettes just seem to *serve*? It's not only about having the best tailor. It is about using clothing like polish on a diamond to help you to shine.

Iris van Herpen is a fashion designer renowned for her intricate, sculptural designs that often incorporate elements inspired by natural forms and mathematical principles. I had the privilege of collaborating with her for the 2022 Met Gala with superstar Dove Cameron. That year the theme was "In America: An Anthology of Fashion." If you don't recall, Dove shone literally as if she were carved into the dress. It was a sculptural masterpiece, featherweight, completely out of this world. Overall, van Herpen's work exemplifies how clothing can be a second skin, an extension of the body that expresses complex ideas about structure, fluidity, and connection. When fashion becomes connective tissue to our outside world is truly when we become next level. Laura Day echoed this thought in our conversation, as she kept bringing up the idea of *unity*—the idea that we are meant to be ourselves in the company of others, not in a vacuum. We give and receive constantly, including with the beauty we bring to the world.

Another designer who deeply understood this was Issey Miyake, whose innovative pleating techniques and architectural forms celebrated the body's movement and the interplay of fabric and space. I have a Danish friend who works in design whose closet is composed almost entirely of pleated Issey Miyake suits in pieces (for travel and for every day). These pieces serve: They literally never wrinkle or crunch, and always drape to perfection. It's almost uncanny. Both Issey and Iris, in their unique ways, demonstrate how fashion can move beyond mere covering to become a conscious exploration of form and energy.

Robert Edward Grant, a prominent figure in the study of sacred geometry, explains that these universal patterns are not just external phenomena; they are imprinted within us. Your body, with its unique proportions and energetic centers, is a living blueprint of sacred geometry. When you dress with this awareness, you are honoring that internal harmony.

Here are some ideas on how to integrate sacred geometry into your everyday styling practice, connecting it to your chakras for an even deeper alignment.

Applying Sacred Geometry to Your Style

1. THE GOLDEN RATIO AND BODY PROPORTION

The Golden Ratio (approximately 1.618) is a mathematical proportion found repeatedly in nature, art, and architecture, and it is often considered inherently beautiful and balanced. Lebanese Italian designer Tony Ward's SS24 collection was called The Golden Ratio. The Golden Ratio also taps into the idea of beauty in threes, which is a familiar feng shui practice. One of my clients had a rule with rings: There always had to be an odd number, and three was the goal. We counted it out together every single time.

Χ *Practice*: Stand in front of a mirror and observe your own body. Where does your natural waist fall? How do your limbs proportion to your torso? Are there any natural symmetries, angles, or proportions that your eye is especially drawn to? The

Golden Ratio is expressed on your physical body as thirds: your head and chest, torso, and legs. See what you notice about yours.

X *Try this*: Use clothing to create harmonious proportions that align with the Golden Ratio, aiming for compositions of thirds (rather than halves). For example, if your torso is one unit or one third, a skirt or pant that elongates your legs, giving the appearance of two, will create a visually pleasing balance. For a crop top, this means pairing with high-waisted bottoms, or carefully choosing jacket lengths that divide your body into these ideal segments as you play with combinations of thirds. You can clasp a belt at your waistline over a dress, add a layer (such as a jacket, trench coat, or scarf), tuck your shirt, or play with shoes that add height to create new proportional breaks.

X *Chakra connection*: This practice primarily supports the Solar Plexus Chakra (Third Ego Center) by enhancing your sense of personal power and confidence through visual balance, and the Root Chakra by creating a sense of grounded, stable proportion.

2. SPIRALS AND FLOW (FIBONACCI SEQUENCE)

The Fibonacci sequence is a mathematical sequence in which each number is the sum of the preceding two numbers (0, 1, 1, 2, 3, 5, 8 . . .). In nature, this sequence generates a spiral pattern found in everything from petal arrangements to pinecones, from seashells to galaxies. Even in the human body, we see this sequence reflected in one nose and mouth, two eyes and ears, three segments of head, upper body, and lower body, and three sections on each limb, and five fingers on each hand. In clothing, the Fibonacci sequence translates into drapes, fluid movements, and gradual expansions to evoke natural beauty and composition.

I first got very into Fibonacci back in college when *The Da Vinci Code* was the hottest (most contagious) phenomenon. But director Ron Howard truly knows how to align pop culture with divine possibility, and by now you know I *love* making the aspirational and divine absolutely accessible. And of course the High Renaissance polymath Leonardo da Vinci himself drew upon the Fibonacci spiral to compose some of his most famous masterpieces, as showcased most memorably in *The Mona Lisa*. If she can wear it, so can you!

ℵ *Practice*: Open your closet and observe how fabrics move and drape. Look for garments that have a natural, unforced flow. This demonstrates why effortless, easy styles typically resonate and seem "stylish." Maybe you pull out a more bohemian, trapeze, or free-flowing dress, an oversized knit or cocoon type cape, or even something with pleats or tulle or fringe—textures that really respond to movement.

ℵ *Try this*: Embrace pieces that feature asymmetrical lines, cascading ruffles, or soft gathers that create gentle spirals or dynamic movement. Think about layered pieces where each layer flows into the next. For example, double up your layers for interesting necklines or throw on an unexpected underlay for a pop of lace or color.

ℵ *Chakra connection*: This resonates strongly with the Sacral Chakra (Second Ego Center), promoting creativity, fluidity, and emotional expression. It also connects to the Water Energy element in feng shui, inviting adaptability and depth.

3. PLATONIC SOLIDS AND STRUCTURE

The five Platonic solids (tetrahedron, cube, octahedron, dodecahedron, icosahedron) are foundational geometric forms. In fashion, this translates to clear, defined shapes and structured pieces.

- χ *Practice*: Identify where you desire more structure or definition in your look.
- χ *Try this*: Incorporate garments with strong lines, architectural cuts, or intentional tailoring. This could be a perfectly tailored blazer (cube), a sharply pleated skirt (angles), or a minimalist dress with clean, geometric seams.
- χ *Chakra connection*: This supports the Metal Energy element in feng shui, fostering authority and clarity. It also aligns with the Solar Plexus Chakra for confidence and the Throat Chakra (Fifth Ego Center) for clear expression and leadership.

By weaving these principles of sacred geometry into your daily dressing ritual, you're not just putting on clothes; you're engaging in a conscious act of alignment. You're transforming your wardrobe into a canvas for your highest self.

Earlier in the book we unpacked color and the elements of feng shui with Amanda Gibby Peters. Here we take it a step further by tying these colors into our body's energetic centers so that we can learn how to use the energy of color to activate how we want to feel, to transform how we show up to a moment or circumstance, and to potentially circumvent a bad mood or draining energy. Our body is essentially a computer we have to learn to reprogram and decode. If we can learn to rewire and better understand our tendencies and our thinking as Dr. Swart asked us, we can rewrite what's possible for us over the course of a lifetime. That starts, of course, with every single choice, every single day. You see, thinking intentionally isn't enough. When you can teach yourself to think strategically alongside the intentionality, you are giving yourself the pen to write your own story.

As I backtracked through the catalogue of my career, I realized I had been unconsciously using the CREATE method while I worked alongside super-watt stars and as I eventually got more and more determined to heal my dis-ease to please. As I have become more successful and methodical over the years, creating this method helped me to delineate the magic, so that both you and I can return to it again and again. We all have our magic, written into our bodies within this sacred chakra rainbow. We just didn't have the programming to realize it. Now you do!

I used to separate my work with movie stars from other creative work that interested me, such as writing or using social media as a platform to inspire and guide people. For a time, I thought bringing any attention either to myself or to the greater potential purpose of my work was narcissistic, egoistic, and frivolous. In creating this method, I visualized and realized that the stars (and the stars I work with) can align, that working with people with a platform can and should have a greater purpose, and that by bringing a cohesive method to the world in a beautiful, accessible, practical way offers alignment to my "work selves" and all the roles I play—mother, partner, creator, founder. When we don't unite all the roles of who we are intentionally, we lose the plot. We can't tell the full story of ourselves if our various storylines aren't in conversation! But by uniting these roles instead of separating them, I found a deeply fulfilling integrity that began vibrating throughout my whole life. When we learn to access and align the energy of our body and its divine wisdom, we present *all* of who we are to the world in integrity. The CREATE method reconnected me with the truth that what you wear has the power to tell the story of *you*—of your very being, your very soul to the world.

Chapter Summary

Threading It All Together

Neuroplasticity—your brain's ability to form new neural connections—is the engine powering change in your life. But you can't simply erase negative thought patterns to manifest your dreams; you must create and strengthen new neural pathways through deliberate, consistent practice until they become dominant.

This blending of the spiritual and the scientific has proven results that reach back through the ages. For example, the chakra system represent gateways where your emotional, spiritual, and physical sides coexist.

Leveraging style's power comes, in part, from aligning fashion's pragmatic aspects (silhouette, proportion, color, fabric) with your energy centers. You can amplify your essence by aligning your fashion choices not only with your physical body but with your energetic body, too.

Quick Alterations to Make

✗ **Practice daily energy alignment.** Stand before your closet, take a breath, and connect with your intention for the day while moving through the seven ego centers. This can be a relatively quick process and will speed up over time.

✗ **Match chakra energy to your day.** Need stability? Choose Root Chakra pieces—structured trousers, chunky boots, military jackets. Need creativity? Embrace Sacral Chakra flow—flowing dresses, wide-leg pants, soft knitwear. Need power? Go Solar Plexus—belted blazers, strong shoulders, fitted silhouettes that highlight your core.

✗ **Experiment with fabric frequencies.** Notice how different fabrics affect your energy levels and mood. Try incorporating more natural fibers (linen, wool, organic cotton) when you need to feel uplifted. Pay attention to when certain fabrics leave you feeling uncomfortable or drained.

✗ **Use color strategically.** Align colors with chakra energy: reds and earth tones for grounding, oranges for creativity, yellows for confidence, greens for compassion, blues for expression, indigos for intuition, violets for spiritual connection. Match colors to the feelings you want to activate.

Continue Designing Your Future

Keep developing a practice of conscious energy alignment that transforms getting dressed into a powerful act of self-harmony. Each morning, trust your inner wisdom to guide you to areas that need attention. Some days you'll focus on one or two centers; other days you'll flow through all seven. Don't worry—this practice will become increasingly intuitive. Pick up one of Laura Day's books, such as *The Prism*, to better understand energy centers.

Understanding that clothing speaks a language others read and respond to, and because of that, creates energy exchanges, is game changing. It forces you to consider both the "inside way" (internal feeling) and "outside way" (external energy) of each garment choice, recognizing that their responses become part of *your* experience.

Over time, by accessing your body's divine wisdom through the chakra system, sacred geometry, and fabric frequencies, you'll present all of who you are to the world, in integrity.

Truth

LIVING IN INTEGRITY TO BUILD
THE BRAND OF *YOU*

"The most important
relationship in life is the one
you have with yourself.
Once you have that, every
other relationship is a luxury."

DIANE VON FÜRSTENBERG

The core function of this book is to help you use your style to broadcast your authentic self and to magnetize what you want most in life. To be sure, magnetism comes from living in complete alignment with who you are—a gravitational pull that draws people, opportunities, and experiences into your orbit. Legendary fashion designer Diane von Fürstenberg (DVF) understood this intuitively. Miraculously, she was born just eighteen months after her mother narrowly escaped dying in a concentration camp during the Holocaust. Diane transmuted her family's legacy into a global fashion empire that celebrates women's vulnerability, strength, and resilience.

I spoke with the fabulous DVF in the thick of summer. At the time, she was aboard the yacht on which she and her husband, business tycoon Barry Diller, were traveling the world (location unknown!). She's created a beautiful, interesting life for herself—and she's done it with unsurpassed intentionality and integrity. When I say unsurpassed, I'm not kidding. DVF told me that in her seventy-eight years, she's never lied. She didn't say it boastfully; she stated it more as fact—the foundation upon which she's built everything else. "I don't know why I never lied. I can't remember anyone telling me not to lie," she reflects. "But for whatever reason, I've always been afraid to lie because somehow I thought it would bring bad luck." Then she joked that she's "100 percent unblackmailable."

I was so charmed by our conversation; DVF has that effect on people. It's not an overstatement to say she's an icon—both in what she's accomplished in fashion and in how she lives her life. She embodies living in integrity, which is really the coherence between your inner truth and your outer expression. When these elements sync, you become irresistible—not because you're trying to be, but because authenticity is naturally magnetic.

Diane says she is "not particularly interested in fashion per se, but I am very interested in being a woman, in having the advantage of being a woman, in knowing what it means to be a woman." It's perhaps a surprising statement not to be interested in fashion for fashion's sake, but I relate to this, because it's always the thing underneath the thing that interests me—the underlying story. No doubt there are experts out there who know way more than I do—an encyclopedic knowledge of fashion history and an in-depth understanding of fabric types, textile production, and more. That's not my jam. My love of fashion stems from its magic—its ability to change our lives and what we deem possible for ourselves.

Womanhood has many dimensions—and that's what makes it fun. Your clothes become an extension of your truth rather than a costume you wear and then take off at the end of the day. In our conversation, DVF identified four essential attitudes that are facets of womanhood that she relates to.

Boss Lady is about channeling confidence and authority without losing your femininity. It's structured shoulders and quality fabrics that move with purpose. It's knowing you belong in that boardroom, that meeting, that negotiation—not because you're pretending to be someone else, but because you're fully inhabiting who you are. When I heard DVF put it this way, I instantly recognized this attitude in myself. When I am in work mode, Boss Lady is always present and serving.

Off Duty maintains your essence even when you're not "on." It's the recognition that your authentic self doesn't clock out. Even in your most casual moments, there's an intentionality to how you present yourself to the world. Personally, I love getting intentional for a morning coffee run or a school drop-off. It doesn't mean going fancy; it means adding something that offers a lift, a little elevation, a bit of pep to your step—elegance, effortless, and easy (my three go-to vibes) work even when you are off duty. Sometimes it's as simple as a "fashion" Birkenstock, an extra-large men's shirt over shorts, an oversized faux fur jacket or sunglasses, or a chunky clog. I keep easy accessories ready in the coat closet by the door—hats, sunglasses, scarves, and bags—for this reason.

Diva embraces the fluidity of your feminine power. It's about understanding that being flirty, playful, or seductive isn't antithetical to being taken seriously. Diva is probably the territory I have had to expand the most over the years, as this aspect of my femininity definitely took some guts to step into. When you own your femininity, it is pretty astonishing how you instantly step into a more magnetic version of yourself.

Hostess embodies gracious authority, whether you are having friends over for dinner, or just inviting others into your world, whether that is a work situation, social groups, or the neighborhood. It is an inviting energy, generous and accommodating. It's about making space for others while maintaining your own powerful presence.

I'm opposed to narratives that aim to isolate women or box them into roles that reduce their power, influence, and earning potential.

Women are multidimensional. Dichotomous. Contradictory.

Superhuman. I get a charge out of working, and I also love hosting people in my home and following women on social media, such as Nara Smith, who wears couture confections while she cooks intricate dishes, even while pregnant. (She now has four children.) When it comes to channeling hostess energy, you don't have to fit anybody's mold, and you don't have to choose between a feminine or feminist expression.

Diane—another working mother—has kept a diary her entire life to maintain what she calls "the communion with yourself." What a beautiful way to put it, and yet another cue that intentional dressing always starts with deeply interior work, before we ever even approach our closet.

This ongoing dialogue with your true essence helps you discover who you are beneath the layers of conditioning we've spoken about. And that includes embracing your imperfections. "You own your imperfections—they become your asset. You own your vulnerability—you turn it into strength. That is what being in charge is about," says Diane.

DVF says: "You should design your life every day." Your wardrobe is a tool in this daily design process. When you dress with intention—not to impress others or follow trends, but to honor the person you are and the life you're creating—you begin to live by design.

When Diane created the still-iconic wrap dress in 1974, she was designing a garment that resonated with millions of women because it captured the spirit of women's liberation: strong and sexy in equal measure. Her commitment to authenticity rippled outward, creating a movement that was about much more than fashion.

This is the power of living in integrity. It doesn't just transform you; it touches everyone who comes into contact with you. Your authenticity gives others permission to be authentic. Your confidence becomes contagious. Your truth creates space for others to discover their own.

As DVF approaches eighty, she's focused on "polishing the package" she'll leave behind after fifty years in business. To me, her legacy is the example she's set of what it means to live in complete alignment with yourself. In that sense, the brand of *you* isn't always something you create—sometimes, like in Diane's case, it's something you reveal. DVF is proof that when you have the courage to live in complete integrity with who you are, you become irresistible.

I also got to interview Fabiola Beracasa Beckman, a producer who makes films that tell impactful stories, including the inspiring documentary *Diane von Furstenberg: Woman in Charge.* She also happens to be the one with the pinky tattoo.

Fabiola told me she views life as "a big anthropological master class. And one of the things that I started doing at a very young age was noticing qualities in people that I loved and how to incorporate them into myself." One example that came to her mind: Businesswoman and philanthropist Maria-Josée Kravis "really made me feel like what was happening in my life was important to her," says Fabiola, who was wowed by such a busy, influential person being so present in their conversation, even when she was still a young girl. "I remember that very day thinking, '*I want to be like that.*'"

This approach extends to negative observations: "When you see qualities in people that you *don't* like . . . it's a trigger. It's a red flag," says Fabiola. "You want to ask yourself, 'Can I try to do that less? Can I be more aware of that?' to get clear about how what you want to communicate to the world by editing yourself through the experience that you have with others."

When we spoke, Kerry Washington was pondering what it means to dress authentically, especially across different life phases. She was remembering how, in high school, she toggled between two vastly different worlds: living in the Bronx and commuting to Spence, a posh private school on Manhattan's Upper East Side. (Fun fact: Gwyneth Paltrow was her schoolmate there.) "I began to kind of understand that fashion was an expression of identity at that young age," remembers Kerry. "There were things that you could say about yourself through what you wore. You could be communicating geography, class, religion, sexuality, confidence."

Kerry had to confront the inherent style dichotomy of living in two worlds and decided: "I was neither just Upper East Side nor just the Bronx. I was both," she said. "Both of those worlds were mine, and I belonged in both of them." So she developed her own "secret style sauce" that honored both aspects of her identity—a style she describes as "both classic and funky."

At another juncture, when she became a mom, Kerry didn't just abandon her previous fashion choices. Instead, she asked: "How does this new part of my identity add a new dimension?"

Women often get confused about who they are after becoming a mom. Maybe you can relate? Every time I was pregnant and also every time after giving birth, I was back to Chapter 1: "Why You Don't Know What the Eff to Wear." Whenever we add another role to the list of roles, it clouds the water a little. This is where getting back to intentionality and revisiting the CREATE method is so handy. Birthing a new you requires you to adapt and allow this newer version of you to emerge.

Practicing Honest Self-Assessment

Another thoughtful woman I admire is designer Aurora James, founder of Brother Vellies—a globally recognized luxury accessories brand that celebrates traditional African design techniques while providing sustainable economic opportunities for artisans. In 2020, Aurora launched Fifteen Percent Pledge, an initiative that calls on major retailers to commit fifteen percent of their shelf space to Black-owned businesses (reflecting the proportion of the Black population in America).

When I asked her for her thoughts on dressing intentionally, she said, *"We are all creating the world we will exist in."* Her approach transcends mere aesthetics; it's about creating a life of integrity where your external choices reflect your deepest beliefs.

Admittedly, that is harder to do in our attention economy, where every choice is amplified. But Aurora reminds us that we're constantly investing in our future reality: "If we shop fast fashion, follow celebrities we deem toxic, keep buying sugary snacks we are continuing to invest in creating that world." Can't argue with that.

Your closet is a daily referendum on your values—and your style reflects that. Aurora asks: "Are you wearing a piece of clothing because it speaks to who you are, or because someone else told you it was what you needed to be wearing?" she finds the latter "extremely boring," and insists that authentic style emerges from your direct connection to yourself.

So how do you distinguish between forcing a look someone else deemed cool and intentionally curating one? Aurora seeks alignment, asking simply: "Does it feel natural to you or forced?" During one of her most creative periods, she wore mostly jeans and vintage T-shirts daily, but animated her look through carefully chosen accessories. The creativity wasn't rooted in complexity; it was in *authenticity*. As we evolve, Aurora suggests, we should "bend less with the wind of trends and become more deeply rooted in our sense of self." Her personal current litmus test: "Will I be excited to wear this for the next ten years?" It's a question that cuts through impulse and gets to the heart of what truly resonates with your soul.

Building an intentional wardrobe requires what Aurora calls "honest self-assessment"—a willingness to examine not just what you own, but why you own it. This honesty extends to acknowledging when you're out of alignment. Aurora admits she's someone who tries to live according to her stated values, emphasizing the word *tries*.

Unsurprisingly, Aurora considers herself a "manifesting generator," someone who wakes up "incredibly grateful to have the life I have." But her approach to manifestation is grounded in action and reciprocity. When you believe something is happening, you act differently than when you think it *might* happen.

Your daily dressing ritual can become a practice of cultivating possibility and wonder. Aurora begins each morning by considering her day's purpose, her location, and her emotional state. Is it a day for playfulness or practicality? Will she be changing clothes frequently at a flea market, or presenting in a corporate boardroom? Each consideration informs her choices.

For inspiration, she imagines vintage pieces' previous lives: where they traveled, who wore them, what stories they carry. She plays with unexpected pairings, letting different decades collide in her wardrobe: Elsa Peretti and Phoebe Philo. Mugler and Melitta Baumeister. Sometimes she reimagines her entire closet "as a Tim

Walker set," approaching getting dressed as a form of creative expression. For the unfamiliar, Tim Walker's signature style is defined by fantastical, dreamlike narratives, in which he blends elaborate, in-camera constructed sets with whimsical costumes and a very specific, sepia-toned color palette to create imaginative scenes that blur the lines between fashion, fine art, and storytelling. His photos evoke both dark fantasy and romantic fairy tales, often incorporating surprising or seemingly random references and a sense of nostalgic, childlike innocence. He is one of my very fave fashion storytellers. Some of my favorite tales include a plane crashing into a bedroom and a giant doll (literally a giant) all dressed up in the forest—literally no rules, which always feels like a relief when I am looking to fashion or fashion photos to get inspired. It makes me think outside of the box, just as I did when I was a little girl.

Manifestation is all about aligning what you desire with how you FEEL

DESIGN YOUR FUTURE

Emma Grede

Business mogul Emma Grede, co-founder of several billion-dollar companies (Skims, Good American, Safely), chairwoman of Fifteen Percentage Pledge, and the first Black woman to be a *Shark Tank* investor, is a fountain of motivational information and one of the freshest voices and thinkers I've come across in the recent past. I also love that she speaks the language of manifestation and energy. Emma embodies a blend of grit, groundedness, and dream chasing that appeals to me, so I wanted to distill some of her wisdom here, about building the authentic brand of *you*.

Nobody Else Is You—Embrace That

Emma is clearly not into creating a faux persona. Something her mother told her—"You are not better than anybody else, but nor is anyone better than you"—became the bedrock of how Emma shows up in every room, every meeting, every moment. "I know my gifts, I know my strengths, and I know that whatever it is that any of us has to bring is valuable," Emma asserted on an episode of Mel Robbins's podcast.[1] "You have to believe that you have something special, unique . . . so make the most of it, figure it out, package it up, and go in with some confidence that at least there's just not another you, right?"

I'll add that the success of Good American, a clothing brand dedicated to size inclusivity, stems in large part because their fans feel seen and heard, and no doubt has to do with Emma's ability to empathize with women who feel underrepresented. Emma has said: "When you have a brand that has a set of beliefs and a purpose, you can't just stick that together with somebody that can't authentically back up that message."[2] Emma's personal values align with her business values—there's no dissonance. "Your brand should reflect the real you."[3]

Be Proud to Take Pride

Have you ever heard the phrase *How you do anything is how you do everything?* Emma subscribes to that—and so do I. I love it and live it and whisper it to my husband at inopportune moments like when I don't like the way the groceries are unpacked and put away. It's that old integrity compass. That's not to say you need to be perfect all the time. But striving for a certain standard with consistency and feeling good about the effort you're putting in—whether that's making your bed or making your tenth cold call of the day for a sales job—can be its own satisfaction.

"There is some kind of invisible magnetic pull to excellence," Emma observes.[4]

Says Emma: "I feel like I'm in practice to be the woman that I want to be constantly."[5]

Tune In to the Energy You Broadcast

When you intentionally choose your self-worth, it emits a positive attitude that reflects that worth to others. "The vibration within you literally changes," Emma says.[6] When you choose to value yourself and recognize the inherent value in others, "You vibrate a different energy."[7]

And when things go sideways in your world, Emma believes that the differentiator between someone who folds and someone who soars is assuring yourself that you are "exactly where I need to be because I'm going to have those [bad] days."[8]

Reward Requires Emotional Risk and Action

If you believe in energy and manifestation, as Emma and I both do, then you know you need to direct your thoughts so that they don't derail your drive to go after what you want. "You have to get out of your head. You have to change the narrative that fills you with the fear that stops you from moving," Emma also told Mel. "You can't think your way into what you want. You can't wish it. You can't hope for it. You got to do."[9] This action-oriented philosophy echoes what Marie Forleo told me. For the specific steps on how to get started, revisit Chapter 3!

Use Style to Uplevel Your State of Mind

But what makes Emma so brilliant is her intimate understanding of the fundamental function clothes serve in our lives. She told NET-A-PORTER: "Through experiences like Good American and Skims, I've also come to understand how closely confidence and self-expression are tied to what we wear."[10]

So what does Emma pull out of her own closet? "I dress entirely to please myself," she's said unapologetically. "Depending on the day, that could be for comfort, or convenience, or because I want to feel bad ass." She has admitted, "I wear the same thing all the time, and I still have that dress-up-for-work mentality. I love a good suit. I love a power shoulder. I buy classic things that I wear over and over again, then I jazz it up with great shoes and handbags. That's where I let the trends come in, but I'm not the trendy, trendy girl."[11]

I pay attention to trends, but it's the intention behind the styling that is always my touchstone. The kind of work I do with actors wouldn't make sense if it was rooted only in trends and how they need to feel, and what kind of idea of themselves they want to share with the public. Awards season is basically a series of appearances and awards from January to March when films and the actors and production involved garner support for nominations from Golden Globes, SAG awards, Oscars, BAFTAs, Emmys, and more. To me, it is essential on those occasions for my clients to "dress like stars." What does that mean? Fashion that doesn't distract or overtake, but that helps the talent shine. This is intentional and tends to garner attention, respect, and more opportunities.

In 2025 *Forbes* discussed my work with Selena Gomez for the press tour of the film *Emilia Pérez* in an article highlighting a return to classic Hollywood style. I talked about our style inspirations and touchstones, saying, "I think anytime one has the opportunity to be in these rooms, to be nominated or in the company at these giant award shows, that's a huge responsibility. And I feel like, as an artist, you really want to shine as your best self. That's the point, right? With Selena, being nominated for this film and it being such a huge, pivotal moment in her career and her life, I think we were just reaching for what would be the most elevated, aspirational, elegant way to tell this story that would best serve in helping her to shine. That was always the purpose."[11]

Every morning presents an opportunity to dress to shine, to win, to vote for the world you want to create. Again, Aurora says it's about trying, about taking "slow steps and fumbles" toward a life of greater alignment. Emma offers that "failure isn't the opposite of success, it's the blueprint for it." Building the brand of *you*, deciding how to present yourself will come through a process of trial and error.

Aurora offered so many pearls of wisdom, but this one has to be my favorite: "Sometimes your best mode of transportation is a leap of faith."

Building the brand of *you* through intentional dressing requires that same faith—in your instincts, in your values, and in your power to create change in your life one choice at a time.

How Integrity Sets You Up to Shine

In 2013, Samira Nasr, my former boss when I was assisting freelance fashion editors, and now *Harper's Bazaar* editor-in-chief, introduced me to Kerry Washington just as I was launching my own freelance styling career. Kerry was looking for someone with great style sense to help her tackle her closet cleanout. I said yes with faith (or at least hope) that I could parlay the job into something more.

Kerry was preparing for an international press tour for Quentin Tarantino's *Django Unchained* with Jamie Foxx, followed by press for her upcoming show, *Scandal*, which she wasn't sure would survive past one season. We all know how that turned out: *Scandal* killed it for seven amazing seasons, and her character, Olivia Pope, became a TV and style icon.

I told her my real line of work was styling actors for red carpets and asked if she'd give me a chance. Thankfully she said yes, which gave my career a major boost. Our fashion collaboration led to me being signed by the Wall Group, the premier agency for stylists and behind-the-scenes creatives. As *Vanity Fair* reported in January

2013: "On the worldwide press tour for 2012's *Django Unchained*, Washington solidified her place in the fashion world's upper crust."

I've watched clients transform how they view themselves as they become more intentional about what they wear. Kerry has a bold, fearless fashion side of her that was waiting for the right moment to emerge. Once she stepped into owning those daring choices—like the Giles Deacon pony-covered white gown we chose for the UK *Django* premiere or the sheer blush Miu Miu dress that was covered in crystals for the 2014 Golden Globes—she shined brighter than ever before. It was extremely intentional, all of it.

What followed was a meteoric rise in her star power: Brand collaborations and ambassadorships materialized, and magazine covers followed. She had unleashed something that was always part of her—and the world took notice. For me, it was a turning point in solidifying that fashion can have a transcendent effect.

Kerry is such a crystal-clear example of how, when you operate in integrity, aligning every choice with your essence, you thrive, you grow, you shine. For stars like Kerry and others, attracting bigger brand deals or more fashion cred is the ripple effect of the joy that aligned style can bring to the fore. And what a joy and a privilege it is for me to be part of that process. I can't explain it better than I did in 2023 when *The Financial Times*, a prestigious British newspaper, ran a flattering article titled: "Superstylist Erin Walsh Can Turn a Star's Style Around."

In the interview I said, "Fundamentally, what I'm here for is to help people better tell their stories through clothes. I'm not in the business of putting my vision on to somebody. I'm helping translate a vision, whether it is a fashion vision or a feeling vision."[12] The piece mentions how generating the right image can meaningfully impact an actor's opportunities, which of course is true. But the force that manifests those opportunities has more to do with the actor's core truth being embodied than about manufacturing a preconceived image.

Women's Wear Daily (WWD) asked me about summoning the powerful within through style in a 2024 article that touted: "Anne Hathaway Enters Her 'Queen Era,' Reprising Iconic Roles and Cementing Her Reign in Fashion."

I said: "One thing that I love about Annie is she has this thing where I think she's learned how to be completely vulnerable and transparent and authentic about who she is. If you look at a Versace woman, always very powerful. That works for Annie because not only is she not afraid to be completely raw, completely real, but with anything she does, she does 600 percent. With these kinds of campaigns, it's about being both. It's the dichotomy of being brave and vulnerable enough to share your real self and all of that person, and I think that's why it works."[13]

That's the core: You gotta be real.

The CREATE method highlights the importance of integrity, with vulnerability being an essential part of tapping into your power. You don't need to be Anne Hathaway to tap into your integrity, but you do need to be willing to do the work, and to get real so you can speak and show your truth.

It would be remiss to discuss the art of building an authentic brand in the style realm and not include Rachel Zoe in the conversation.

"Style is a way to say who you are without having to speak— your wardrobe is this narrative," says fashion editor, stylist, and entrepreneur Rachel Zoe, who understands this concept intimately.

Her philosophy takes the daily act of getting dressed from a mundane routine into an intentional practice of self-expression and empowerment.

Says Rachel: "Every piece you own should evoke a memory, a feeling, a mood, or a dream version of yourself that you're stepping into." It's about curating experiences. The magic lies in understanding how different pieces affect your internal state. Gold lamé and sequins might make you feel glamorous and undeniably yourself, while a flowing caftan channels ease and grace. Maybe it's as simple as a great reliable vintage jean that makes you happy, or monochrome looks that offer you a sense of polish, or maybe you feel most yourself in a classic trench coat or little black dress, or maybe you come alive in maximalist color and prints that really ask you to step up to the moment and take a risk. These aren't arbitrary associations; they're personal truths that help you access different facets of your identity.

"Aspirational dressing" often gets misunderstood as pretending to be someone you're not. Rachel reframes this beautifully: It's not about becoming someone else, but about "becoming the most elevated version of yourself." Start with one piece that inspires you. Build from there, allowing that initial spark to guide the rest of your choices.

In an industry that can reward ruthlessness, Rachel has built her success on a foundation of kindness without sacrificing strength. She learned from watching her father build a successful business while leading with confidence and never compromising his kindness. "You can be powerful, respected, and successful—without ever stepping on anyone to get there," she says, adding that true strength is "knowing who you are and staying true to that—always."

It's actually something I am asked all the time: how to be kind or even nice and manage to lead and get things done at the same time. I find it is much easier to lead from a place of calm, kindness, and clarity, grounded in the confidence that there is truly room for all kinds of people and all kinds of style. I have learned over the years that kindness isn't compromising to excellence; I actually find it to be a secret shortcut to true excellence. Compassion is just about having the courage to get straight to the point—operating in integrity with yourself and with others, in all situations. Even style comes from the courage to have compassion for yourself. When Rachel presented me with Style Curator of the Year in 2024 at the Daily Front Row Los Angeles Fashion Awards, she sweetly said that my magnetism comes from leading from my heart. Is there any other way?

Surrounded by strong women who taught her to block out toxicity, Rachel understands that "protecting your energy is everything." You can't avoid all criticism, but you can discern what deserves your attention and what should be deflected.

Your Story, Your Style

Ultimately, building the brand of *you* through intentional dressing is about recognizing that every day offers a new opportunity to tell your story. Your wardrobe becomes the vocabulary, your styling choices the syntax, and your confidence the voice that brings it all together. When you dress with intention, honoring both your authentic self and your highest aspirations, you create a powerful narrative that speaks before you ever say a word. As Miuccia Prada famously said: "Fashion is instant language."[14]

Conveying an essence is what drives the business of branding. Over the years I have worked with countless agencies and people involved in branding: creative directors, advertising agencies, public relations firms, brand incubators, talent business development firms, you name it. Whether you are a luxury brand or a sustainable new startup, perception matters.

And so do authenticity and believability. For a consumer to want to buy something from a brand, they have to believe what is being said, shown, and sold is true. When it comes to telling your story in style, you have to first believe in that story yourself. And when you do, new possibilities and plotlines begin to emerge.

Chapter Summary

Threading It All Together

Magnetism comes from living in complete alignment with who you are—a gravitational pull that draws people, opportunities, and experiences into your orbit. This coherence between your inner truth and outer expression becomes irresistible because authenticity is naturally magnetic.

Women are multidimensional, dichotomous, contradictory, superhuman—you don't have to choose between feminine and feminist expression.

Quick Alterations to Make

✗ **Practice honest self-assessment.** Go through your closet and ask Aurora James's questions: "Does this speak to who I am, or did

someone else tell me I needed it? Does it feel natural or forced?"
Remove anything that doesn't pass this test.

✗ **Notice qualities you admire in others.** Like Fabiola Beracasa
Beckman, observe the qualities you love in other people and
embody those qualities in your own, always-genuine way. Also
notice what behavior in others triggers you negatively—it may be
revealing what you want to edit in yourself.

✗ **Design your life daily.** Following Emma Grede's approach,
consider your day's purpose, location, and emotional state each
morning. Is it a day for playfulness or practicality? Let each
consideration inform your choices.

Continue Designing Your Future

Cultivate what Diane von Fürstenberg calls "communion with
yourself"—an ongoing inner dialogue with your true essence.
Embrace your so-called imperfections as assets. There is not another
you—that is your superpower.

The truth is you gotta be real. Building an authentic brand—the
brand of you—requires vulnerability as an essential part of tapping
into your power. When you operate in integrity and make every
choice in alignment with your very best essence, you will grow and
thrive.

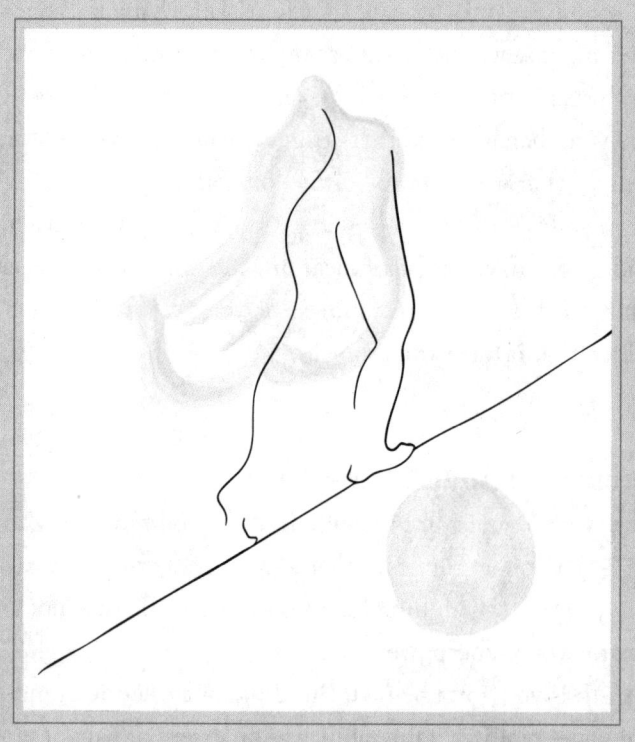

Expansion

TESTING YOUR OWN BOUNDARIES
TO OPEN NEW POSSIBILITIES

"Personal style is about taking
a risk, trying something
unexpected, and having fun
with fashion, but always
being true to yourself."

RALPH LAUREN

Jennifer Hyman **never set out** to revolutionize how women think about risk. Yet as the brilliant co-founder and CEO of Rent the Runway—the groundbreaking company that created what Jenn calls "the closet in the cloud"—she's discovered something profound about the relationship between fashion experimentation and personal evolution. Her company, which gives women access to designer clothes through a subscription rental model, has become far more than a business innovation. It's become a laboratory for understanding how fashion risk and experimentation can transfer to other aspects of our lives.

When we stop seeing fashion as frivolous or beyond our reach, we can better harness its transformative power. Historically, having expendable income created permission to fail and, sometimes also, permission to grow. "If you have a very limited budget, you're going to play it safer. You're going to stick to what you know, what is more ordinary, what is more basic because the actual financial and emotional cost of failing is so high," says Jenn.

That's why democratizing fashion risk isn't just about clothes— it's about creating a practice ground for growth. Sure, having more spending ability can empower you to take risks in your personal style, but it's not the only way. Great creativity is also empowered through constraints, when we learn to use what we have to style new possibilities, and growth can happen here, too. When we remove the financial barrier to experimentation, something magical happens: We begin to remember that change is not only possible, but it can be enjoyable!

No story illustrates this better than the founding moment of Rent the Runway itself. Jenn recalls the pop-up shop that launched the vision: "These two girls came into the pop-up. They saw this one dress that was super popular at the time from across the room. They ran over to the dress. In the middle of one-hundred-plus people, one of the girls stripped. She put on this dress and everything about her changed. Her expression changed. Her body language changed. She stood up straighter. She threw her hair back. She threw her shoulders back. And she turned to her friend and she was like, 'I look so hot.'"

This moment crystallized everything for Jennifer and her co-founder, Jennifer Fleiss, who had been her roommate at Harvard. Jenn says, "That's the feeling that I've seen millions of times since we started the business and that's the feeling that's fueled me . . . you can see this change from head to toe in someone's energy. They feel it right away and they exude it right away."

I said at the outset this book is for every level of earner. That may mean finding creative solutions to economic barriers (such as permission to experiment) so they *don't* inhibit you from taking risks or limit your capacity for growth. Here are a handful of creative solutions:

1. **Get a subscription to Rent the Runway.** Access luxury and special occasion pieces by renting them. This tip feels particularly genuine for me because for clients in the spotlight, I have the advantage of being able to pull new samples from designer collections—and like for Cinderella, they go back directly after usually. Rent the Runway gives you the luxury of a limitless closet in the cloud with zero culpability. You can try it all and mix it up and exponentially expand your closet, make an actual runway in

there while you're at it, while feeling completely held and at ease that you are not beholden to any of it. Risk with reward. It is very genius. They keep getting better and better.

2. **Trade with your circle.** Organize regular exchanges where everyone brings pieces they've outgrown or no longer wear. It's giving community and sustainability! A win-win evening would be akin to a potluck: Have a girls' night where everyone brings two or three quality pieces that they no longer have use for. Everyone trades; everyone wins. Fashion should be a way to commune with your people. This allows for a bit of expansion and it's actually sustainable.

3. **Shop your own closet.** Before adding anything to the cart, spend time remixing existing pieces, as part of the "joy exercise" suggested by Zac Posen in Chapter 5. AI-powered apps, like Doji, are now making this even easier. You can literally try things on without trying them on. The future will be about uploading your closet and being pointed to what's missing, including being directed to where to get a missing piece in the marketplace at any price point, like with the app One Off. Cher's computerized closet from *Clueless* is no longer just a dream.

4. **Build your capsule wardrobe slowly.** Invest in one high-quality, versatile piece per quarter. Focus on items that can be styled multiple ways and transition across seasons. Even when you have access to Rent the Runway, you still need a base wardrobe, and it's smart to think of one to five pieces per season that might need an update. Plenty of retailers are not price gouging and offer takes on designer-inspired styles for less. Aritzia, for one, has been masterful at offering price friendly options to *all* the roles we play,

especially working women who don't want cookie-cutter corporate options. And Zara is the go-to for every single stylish fashion assistant I have ever met.

5. **Master the secondhand market.** Shop pre-loved designer, vintage, and other pieces for less through platforms like Vestiaire, Poshmark, ThredUp, and The RealReal. Or hit up your local consignment store where you can sell pieces you've outgrown to fund new additions. Because many trends are resurrections from the past, you will definitely be able to find "cousins" of new trends in a place that stocks the original pieces that inspired them.

6. **Shop strategically.** Think end-of-season sales, Black Friday, Amazon Prime Day, and designer outlet stores. When I first got into fashion, sample sales were my saving grace.

The Cascade Effect: From Closet to Life

When we give ourselves permission to experiment with presentation, the halo effect extends far beyond our wardrobes. "I feel like you go after life in a completely different way," says Jenn. "And going after it isn't just about your career or your job . . . it's in every realm, like the adventures you go on, the friends that you meet, the conversations you end up having, the fun you end up having."

Democratizing risk in fashion democratizes risk everywhere else, because when we practice courage in small, manageable ways, that builds our capacity for bigger leaps.

Another Jennifer in my life is the embodiment of risk-taking in fashion and life. I'm talking about the one and only Jennifer

Fisher. Over the years, I've watched her transform from a stylist to a jewelry designer to an empire builder, cookbook author, and lifestyle mogul—all while never losing her authentic self. I've witnessed how her approach to taking calculated risks has allowed her to continuously evolve into who she's meant to be. One pivotal example: She wore the custom charm necklace she made on set as a stylist one day even though "until then, charms were only for bracelets and some people thought it was weird," says Jennifer. But when the hairstylist on set that day saw it, he wanted one for actress Uma Thurman. The day Uma received it, she wore it on the cover of *Glamour* magazine, which effectively launched the Jennifer Fisher jewelry brand. She took a risk that felt right to her and it paid off—big time.

Jen is one of the most hilarious, generous women I know, and I'm fortunate to call her a close friend. She's someone who truly shows up for other women—whether offering birthing advice or, memorably, messengering a diamond necklace with an "M" for my newborn Matilda to Lenox Hill Hospital when she was just two hours old.

Jen has an intuitive gift for knowing what people need before they know it themselves, a quality that serves both her friendships and her ability to anticipate what customers didn't know they wanted until she creates it for them. Any time with Jen guarantees laughter until it hurts, usually because she's brazenly honest about truths most people spend energy avoiding.

Whether she's thrown into the deep end of a situation or jumps in voluntarily, Jen always seems to find her way. I asked her how she does it. She said, "The only way to know is to do." Those words perfectly encapsulate her philosophy when it comes to both style and life. "You learn and you realize from all the things you do what you *should* be doing," says Jen.

This mindset applies to how we approach our personal style. So often, women tell me they're afraid to try new looks, worried they'll make the wrong choice or look ridiculous. But what if we reframed this fear? What if we saw every outfit as an experiment and every style choice as valuable data about who we're becoming?

The Evolution of Self-Expression

Jen has gone through countless style iterations over the years—platinum hair, maximalist jewelry moments, bohemian eras. But here's what I find remarkable: She speaks of each phase with respect and gratitude. "I wouldn't be who I am now if I hadn't gone through that phase," she reflects. "That's who I was at the time, and you don't want to regret that." Well said.

So instead of cringing at past fashion choices or dwelling on all of the reasons we went over in Chapter 1 about why we don't know what the eff to wear, let's honor them as necessary steps in our evolution.

I, for one, had a *Sex and the City* phase during my college years in New York City in the early aughts; I reenacted every zany outfit legendary stylist Patricia Field dreamed up for Carrie Bradshaw—tutus, nameplate necklaces, headscarves, skyscraper stilettos, you name it. I stand by this era, tutus and all! I believe it helped me attract Sarah Jessica Parker as a client years later. I had certainly done the "embodying the feeling" part of the manifestation puzzle. That's just one example from my history of phases; I'm sure you have yours, and I want you to own them with total conviction. Each phase teaches us something about ourselves: what makes us feel powerful, what feels authentic, what no longer serves us.

Mindy Kaling articulates this evolution: "In my thirties I had a different body shape. I, for whatever reason, gravitated more towards bodycon and color," she says. "I used to wear stilettos almost exclusively. In my forties my taste has changed . . . I think you've been someone who has really unlocked my love of a really gorgeous flat."

The point is: Give yourself permission to experiment without the pressure of finding your "forever" style. Style is meant to be dynamic. When we lock ourselves into rigid boxes of who we think we should be—at any given time—we deny ourselves the opportunity for continual growth and self-discovery.

Jen's approach to getting dressed is both strategic and experimental. "I keep a rack in my room of unworn looks," Jen explained. It's essentially a curated collection of outfit experiments waiting to happen. This is genius because it removes the pressure of having to create something new from scratch when you're feeling a bit more adventurous.

Risk-taking requires experimentation within your own boundaries. I use Michael Kors's "guardrails" strategy from Chapter 5; risk for risk's sake rarely feels rewarding. So I create parameters: If I'm wearing something more revealing than usual, I ensure it's secure and prep my body with movement earlier so I feel confident. For avant-garde silhouettes or unexpected choices, I pair them with chunky platforms that make me feel empowered and closer to the gods.

As I've gotten older, jewelry has become my preferred playground for bold experimentation without major consequences. I commit to trying what feels new or different to keep expanding my sense of possibility. It's essential for growth. But you'll design your own system that allows calculated risks while keeping you tethered to what makes you feel held and whole.

Here's How You Test Your Own Boundaries

Assemble a risk rack: Even if you don't have one of those free-standing wardrobe racks (or like me, don't want it hanging out in the middle of your bedroom), you can dedicate a section of your closet to combinations you haven't tried yet. This would be a great opportunity to have some Rent the Runway pieces ready to go, and then I would add some pieces that might offer more proportion play: a legging with an oversized blazer, a feminine dress topped with a leather biker jacket, a cropped T-shirt (you can pin or cut one you already have) with high-waisted, wide-leg trousers. A new take on jeans (every season brings a new shape) is a fun way to go. Having these preplanned experiments ready removes the decision fatigue and makes it easier to step up the style risk factor.

Calendar dress: Similarly to interior designer Kelly Wearstler, Jen Fisher says she is "calendar oriented" in her approach to dressing, considering not just her mood but her day's activities. This doesn't mean playing it safe; it means being strategic about when and how you take risks. For Jen, a creative meeting might be the perfect time to try that avant-garde silhouette, while a more corporate presentation might call for a power accessory paired with classic pieces. For someone else, that might be choosing cool tech fabrics for an active day of weekday errands or teaching yoga, and then more artistic, bohemian pieces for a Sunday farmers' market stroll followed by coffee with friends. Start with the essential question "How do I want to feel?" as the through line, and remember that the question might have a different answer for each occasion, so we have to pivot our look essentials accordingly.

Apply the three-look strategy: When Jen has important events, she tries on three different options the night before, knowing each fits differently and will work for different moods or weather or whatever. This prep allows for spontaneity within structure; you can take risks because you've already done the groundwork.

Prep = no regrets: Whether it's having backup options, understanding what works for our body, or simply having the right undergarments, we can be more open about taking risks when we know we won't be left feeling uncomfortable or unprepared.

Honestly, I don't even think "regret" appears in Jennifer Fisher's vocabulary. She is ballsy, but it's not blind bravado. "I fail every day," she admits. "There's something that does not go right in my life every day. So what? Big deal. Okay, that didn't work. Next!"

Though Jen is a master manifester, she doesn't use that exact language herself—and that's okay! You don't have to use spiritual terminology to get what you want. So long as you have faith that what you desire will be yours. When there was "no cool jewelry to wear to represent your kids," she created it with her signature initial charms, which became iconic. When she couldn't find the salt or candles she wanted, Jen got to work. "All of those things didn't really exist in the form that I wanted so I made my own," she explains.

No wonder her personal mantra is "I can fucking do it."

At this stage in her life, with her kids about to leave for college and her business expanding globally, Jen is entering another phase of reinvention. When we chatted, she was launching a men's line, a lifestyle platform called Maedyn, and even considering where she wants to live. This willingness to question and change even the most fundamental aspects of her life demonstrates the kind of radical self-honesty that leads to authentic self-expression. It's never too late to ask: "Does this still serve who I'm becoming?"

In the same vein, your style evolution doesn't end at any particular age or life stage. In fact, I'd argue that the older we get, the more permission we should give ourselves to experiment because we're closer to understanding who we really are beneath the expectations and assumptions.

Jen's most compelling attribute is her allegiance to that truth. She's not trying to fit into someone else's definition of appropriate or attractive. She knows that the willingness to experiment, to fail, and to evolve is what makes you an icon. Clothes (and accessories!) punctuate that status.

Risk and Vulnerability

Self-growth researcher, author, and lecturer Brené Brown has defined vulnerability as "uncertainty, risk and emotional exposure."[1] Fashion is ultimately about being vulnerable because we are sharing ourselves with the world through what we wear.

That said, we want to calculate that exposure. When I've tried a wild fashion idea on a client for the sole reason to do something provocative or boundary-pushing, it usually hasn't worked. But when I push boundaries in the interest of safely coaxing someone out of their comfort zone to expand what's possible for them (roles, brand ambassador opportunities, self-realization), that is the kind of upleveling that makes an impact.

Case in point: For a Bulgari brand event in Rome in May 2024, I had Zac Posen design his first Gap Studio offering—a custom white shirtdress with built-in corset, a modern take on Audrey Hepburn's cult classic *Roman Holiday* style—for Anne Hathaway, Bulgari's brand ambassador. Pairing a seven-figure diamond choker with that Gap Studio shirtdress was a bold risk in a sea of fancy gowns. Anne loved it. She shined from within and sparkled from without. (Gap launched a capsule collection of the dress immediately after, which sold out within hours.) At the event, as we sat for the show, where models and the radiant Isabella Rossellini showcased the brand's newest collection for VIPs and VICs (very important customers), a stylist sitting next to me asked admiringly, "What is Anne wearing??" to which I responded, "Gap." We laughed and both agreed it was fabulous.

Women's Wear Daily and other fashion press praised the look, with *Vogue* noting, "With this extreme approach to high-low dressing, Anne Hathaway took a risk that definitely paid off in our book." This approach also satisfied the all-important "How do you want to feel?" question. For Anne, it was effortless, easy, and elegant—the perfect trifecta.

Expanding Through Structure

I've talked about getting hooked on a feeling when it comes to intentional dressing, and I've definitely gotten hooked on the feeling that Hilary Hoffman's SotoMethod class gives me. It's a killer workout, but it's so much more than that.

I'm sharing this because through SotoMethod, Hilary has taught me about the relationship between structure and freedom. "Imagine if you went to work and your calendar was blank every day. You would spend so much time deciding what to do," says Hilary. "When you've created a road map or a process for yourself, you're free to pour your energy into execution rather than decision-making."

Structure doesn't limit, it liberates.

It's about having the intentionality to show up consistently in order to make the progress you desire. When she was working in the cut-throat (and sometimes soul-sucking) atmosphere of Wall Street, where she was an investment banker, Hilary devised her "51% rule"—the idea that "as long as you can feel inspired fifty-one percent of the time, you're going to keep moving forward."

Adopting this framework gives you permission to acknowledge that not every single day will feel magical—that building something meaningful often requires moving through periods of discomfort. Expansion. The key is to maintain enough inspiration to keep taking that next step.

The other thing that SotoMethod encourages is to celebrate—rather than apologize—for who you are. After years of being told she was "too intense," Hilary made a conscious choice that reverberates through everything she does: "I could either become something that someone wanted me to be, or I could really lean into who I am. . . . I'm an intense person and it's okay. There are people who love that and people who don't. But I'd rather focus on the thing that *I'm* proud of."

Bravo to shedding acquired behaviors, embracing your authentic self, and never shrinking to fit into spaces that were never designed for your full expression. That's what expansion is all about.

A Fashionable Evolution

At this point in our shared journey I hope you embrace fashion for what it truly is: a powerful medium of self-expression, a tool for psychological well-being, and an incredible way to tell the deeper story of who you are becoming. In this context, I say *becoming*—not *are*—intentionally, because expansion requires evolution. It's what makes us interesting beings and it's what makes fashion and dressing fun. It's not static. Not forever.

I've witnessed some truly powerful "fashion" moments over the years. I've been brought to tears watching someone expand into a version of themselves bigger than they ever imagined possible. After I've worked with a client at an awards show, my night ends with me dashing home to watch what I've taken part in unfold, champagne in hand. Selena Gomez presenting at the 2025 Academy Awards? Breathtaking. But what made that moment electric wasn't just the stunning couture Ralph Lauren blush crystal-adorned gown; it was witnessing Selena step fully into her superstar power, at ease, confident, feeling beautiful and whole. Even the Ralph Lauren tailor was weeping.

Fashion *is* powerful. At the 2023 Met Gala, Anne Hathaway transformed into a Chanel–Versace hybrid superwoman. The collaboration between two legendary fashion houses was refreshing and unexpected, just like Anne herself. Watching her float up those Met steps in her white tweed statement cut-out gown, arm-in-arm with Donatella Versace, was an iconic fashion moment.

In 2015, I had five clients at the Met Gala, then went straight to the hospital to give birth to my daughter—my own version of pushing past limits. Leaving the hospital, I wore the sky-blue Manolo Blahnik heels I had worn at my wedding. I was stepping into my most important role yet and I needed to dress the part to recognize this supremely special occasion.

When I first met Anne Hathaway in 2018, she was pregnant with her second son, Jack. We collaborated with Oscar de la Renta to design a gorgeous white sculptured pants look to celebrate her dramatically changed figure. It was fresh and, more importantly, it made her look and feel beautiful, feminine, and powerful for her film premiere of *Modern Love*. The look resonated deeply.

Since then, working with her wildly specific, curious, and intentional spirit has pushed me to ask more of myself. Our professional relationship as well as our friendship has continued to transform my life, which is why this book is full of stories with my beloved Annie, as I call her, and why I asked her to write the foreword to it. Taking the journey with her feels so magical. We aren't thinking small.

My understanding of fashion's transformative power didn't come from nowhere. I vividly remember watching my mother, Jane, get dressed for work every day. She was an appellate attorney with "Diane Lane" look-alike vibes, as one of my uncles tells me, and she made it both a habit and an art to be dressed impeccably every single day: nylons, pumps, and always a put-together, elegant ensemble that

communicated sophisticated Boss Woman. I would watch her transform before heading off to work and then again upon returning home. Jewelry came off first, everything hung up meticulously and returned to its proper place. (She kept all of her shoes in their original boxes for years, like a library, including her wedding shoes, which still had the dime taped in the lining for good luck.) She would take a bath and then put on an evening look. Even if it was pajamas, they were well-kept and put on a refined air. The same art of dressing was applied to evenings out with my dad: She approached it very intentionally. Usually an elevated dress with flattering neckline or a cool blouse/pants look. But I recall the vibe of her choices more than the actual garments. She was (and is) elegant, refined, feminine, beautiful. My mother created a world around the entire process of dressing, and I loved watching it.

As an attorney in rooms full of mostly men, my mother managed to convey her power without sacrificing her femininity. She harnessed it as a superpower and used what she wore to play the part. My grandmother (also named Jane) operated similarly, relying on systems of gorgeous accessories, Chanel and St. John mixed with the label-less as well. She was an early advisor to me that investing in statement accessories was key to grounding your look. She was equally at ease in a thrift store or TJ Maxx as she was in Chanel; it was the quest for the pieces to suit her vibe that thrilled her. She was extremely resourceful at executing a fashion vision, no matter the price point.

Thinking back to her journey, I realize that fashion can be more than just a means of transformation; it can be a means of survival. In the mid-'70s, my grandfather was murdered at his home in Palm Beach. (The details surrounding that family tragedy are a story for another day.) My grandmother had to step into the role of leading his oil company after not having worked in her entire adult life, while also guiding her six children through the crisis.

She described to me how taking over his company required her to channel the person she urgently, unexpectedly needed to be—both in terms of how she felt and also how she presented herself. To her, communicating strength meant being truthful and vulnerable about taking on a role she had no other choice but to play. That integrity and vulnerability became her superpowers—a running theme in this book.

Like my mother (who no doubt learned it from her), my grandmother dressed the part of elegant boss every single day, offering her team (and herself) a believable emblem of confidence through fashion—a myth that became reality. That's perhaps why I was so moved when Diane von Fürstenberg told me she believes "[we] must create a myth of ourselves."

The thing about myths is they are meant to be epic. They're meant to be immersive and expansive. Whenever I have allowed myself to feel small or play small, it has been because I temporarily forgot the narrative I was weaving. This book and the CREATE method can prevent you from ever losing the plot.

So let's break down how to CREATE your own story, your style, your myth in daily life.

Chapter Summary

Threading It All Together

Society would have you believe that experimentation means you're lost and merely putting on costumes. Don't fall for it! As adults, it is our responsibility to evolve over time. The most evolved among us feel comfortable in transformation because we're vulnerable enough to admit: "Who I was yesterday isn't actually who I will be tomorrow. I want to get better."

But pushing boundaries works when it's in the interest of safely moving out of a comfort zone to expand what's possible—not for shock value alone. Expansion requires thoughtful evolution—it's what makes us interesting and dressing fun.

Quick Alterations to Make

✗ **Honor your style evolution.** Instead of cringing at past fashion choices, honor them as necessary steps in your evolution. Each phase teaches something about what makes you feel powerful, what feels authentic, what no longer serves you. Give yourself permission to experiment without pressure of finding your "forever" style.

✗ **Find creative solutions to economic barriers.** Subscribe to Rent the Runway for low-risk experimentation. Organize clothing swaps with friends—everyone brings two or three quality pieces for trading. Shop your own closet using AI-enabled apps to remix existing pieces. Build a capsule wardrobe slowly with one high-quality, versatile piece per quarter. Master the secondhand market through Vestiaire, Poshmark, ThredUp, The RealReal, or local consignment shops.

✗ **Assemble a risk rack.** Dedicate a section of your closet to combinations you haven't tried yet—leggings with oversized blazers, feminine dresses with leather jackets, cropped sweaters with high-waisted, wide-leg trousers. Having pre-planned experiments removes decision fatigue and makes stepping up the style risk factor easier.

✗ **Apply the three-look strategy.** For important events, try on three different options the night before. This prep allows spontaneity within structure—you can take risks because you've done the groundwork. Prep equals no regrets.

Continue Designing Your Future

Expansion will teach you to stop reserving your best self (and clothes!) for "special" occasions. Why limit yourself to feeling extraordinary only on birthdays, anniversaries, vacations, and other events when you could feel this way every day? Every morning when you get dressed you will send yourself the message: "I am worth the effort. I am ready to show up fully for my life."

Practicing courage in small, manageable, fashion-driven ways builds that capacity for bigger leaps—not just in your closet, but in every corner of your beautifully unfolding life.

Using the CREATE Method Every Day

"It's not the big moves that change everything—it's the smallest ones in your everyday life that do."

MEL ROBBINS

When I first sat down to write this book, five words crystallized my vision: *Actionable. Accessible. Elevated. Everyday. Method.* They became the foundation of everything I wanted to share with you.

My approach to fashion has always been a study in balance. I navigate the tension between masculine and feminine, between accessible and elevated, all while maintaining an ease, which is essential to my multihyphenate existence juggling many roles.

None of us feel the same way every day. We need a system that can adapt to our changing selves while remaining grounded in who we truly are.

Many people have asked me: "Do you actually use this method with clients? Do you follow these steps yourself?" The answer is yes—on both counts—but for a lot of my career, I was doing it intuitively.

The CREATE method didn't emerge overnight. It was born from thousands of hours of work, study, research, application, and—*yes*—very public trials and errors. It came from the process of excavating and translating my instinctive practice into teachable, replicable steps.

That's the power of having a clear method: It transforms intuitive knowledge into something you can consciously apply, refine, and share. I know my practice now in a way I never did before. And through the CREATE method, you can develop that same clarity and confidence in yours.

At this point in our journey together, you know the information I share is to help you navigate not just your closet, but your relationship with yourself—unique, imperfect, beautiful, and ever evolving.

Putting the CREATE Method to Work for You

Dressing with intention—that is, dressing with the CREATE method—is about aligning your style with the truth of who you want to be in this world, so you can summon your highest self and make good shit happen.

CLARITY   RITUAL   EDITING   ALIGNMENT   TRUTH   EXPANSION

Consider the **Clarity** step to be the foundation. Get real with yourself. Get clear on your goals in your life, get clear on how you feel (physically and emotionally), and get clear on how you want to feel. Be ruthless in your quest for clarity. Every day you need to ask yourself the hard questions: "How do I feel? How do I want to feel? What do I want to give today? What do I want to receive today?"

Get CALM in your clarity and remind yourself of the steps to get CALM (clarity, assessment, love, mantra). Pick your mantra for the day and lean into it. Get clear on your intention for the day, and make every single thing in every single day rooted in that intention. When you get lost or sidetracked, pause and go back to that intention. Write it down.

For **Ritual**, find tools that help you feel grounded and emotionally aligned. What systems do you step up to unite all your senses so that your body and spirit are working on the same team? As intuitive Laura Day reminded me, "everything in every day can become a ritual if you let it." Rewire what's possible for you every day by firing all your senses as if they were your own personal inspiration army. Use consistency and reflection with ritual to keep you rooted in your intention. As SotoMethod founder Hilary Hoffman shouts in her class, "Consistency is step one. Consistency with reflection is step two." Choose what methods work for you and keep at it. Consistency will rewire what you think is possible for yourself.

When you **Edit** your wardrobe, you **edit** your life. The art of dressing intentionally is rooted in a desire to design your life. You get real with your wardrobe, you edit out what is no longer serving you, and you take the reins in writing the story of how you present yourself to the world. You stop playing the victim of what people think, or what trends tell you you need, because you design your closet so that it is not only your armor to face the world but your portal to possibility. You edit your wardrobe so that every single element in it is reflective of the person you are, the person you are becoming, and the person you want to be. No excuses.

You develop a deeper, more profound appreciation of your body and its potential when you use its energetic systems, chakras, and basic fundamentals to serve how you feel. By learning the very **Alignment** of your body and soul, you work in tandem with your divine design and basic tools like clothing to become truly next level.

An extension of alignment is **Truth**—the element of living in integrity and always reassessing what your truth looks like at various stages of your life. It's freeing to steep yourself in the energies (and outfits) that feel right to you—and you alone.

You **Expand** what's possible for yourself and the world you live in when you deign to dream bigger—to take risks that keep in mind your intention. You push past the self-imposed or given boundaries to become a brighter, more realized version of yourself. Surrender to the ebb and flow of expansion and offer yourself your own safety net as you progress.

Everyday Use of the CREATE Method

Let's do a breakdown of how you might use this book every single day. To integrate the CREATE method into your daily routine, remember that consistency is key. It's not about a one-time fix but a sustained practice that leads to lasting change.

Consistency is key: The CREATE method is most effective when practiced consistently. Just like a workout regimen, daily engagement builds stronger neural pathways and reinforces new habits.

Embrace small steps: You don't have to overhaul your entire closet or your mindset in a single day. Focus on small, manageable actions that align with each step of the method. For example, in your closet, if you are confused, grab three items that make you feel great, or even better, that make you feel how you want/need to feel that day. Recall why these are touchstones and how they make you feel. It's an instant reconnection exercise. This is always a great place to start. The small systems that you make for yourself as a result of this book will change your life when you commit to them.

Cultivate self-awareness: Pay attention to how your clothing choices affect your energy, mood, and confidence throughout the day. This ongoing feedback loop helps you refine your practice. I am deeply attuned to my physical reaction to getting dressed. If something feels off, I move on. You will refine your intuition in this process.

Prioritize and practice grace: Understand that not every day will be perfect. Some days you might focus more on elimination, others on aligning with your chakras. Give yourself grace and focus on the process rather than perfection.

Journal your journey: Keeping a style journal can help you track your progress, note insights, and celebrate small victories. This reinforces positive behaviors and helps you stay motivated.

 By weaving the CREATE method into your daily life, you transform routine acts into powerful opportunities for self-discovery, alignment, and manifestation, consciously shaping the brand of *you* with every choice.

The Digital Revolution in Your Closet

It's an extraordinary time to be alive and getting dressed. The convergence of artificial intelligence (AI) and personal style is opening up even more possibilities. I would never—ever!—tell you to outsource your intuition to a computer model; I'm simply saying that AI could become a valuable partner in unlocking the full potential of your wardrobe.

Jennifer Hyman, founder of Rent the Runway, understands this potential better than most. As she sees it, AI can help solve the "paradox of choice" problem when it comes to style decisions. Her company offers customers access to tens of thousands of items, yet they still struggle with the fundamental question of "I don't know what to pick." Even when presented with "this unlimited closet of fashion, some people don't experience the reckless abandon you might expect," says Jennifer, who attributes that reaction to "this barrier in the female psychology: What if I get it wrong?" Jennifer says that no matter who you are, "eighty percent of the stuff in your closet is really underutilized."

Through apps that digitize your wardrobe, AI innovations can help you wear more of what you already own because they can cut through this psychological paralysis. In a sense, they are stylists in your pocket who can reveal clothing combos you may never have imagined or identify what items are missing to elevate your style story.

The goal isn't to replace your judgment but to help you make peace with experimentation itself so you can move past the fear that keeps you reaching for the same safe choices. That is one of the reasons I am bullish on AI myself.

My advice: Approach these style innovations with curiosity. You'll gravitate to the tools that amplify your natural wisdom rather than replace it. The most transformative AI will be those that help you become fluent in your own style language—not talk over you.

10 NONNEGOTIABLE STEPS TO INCORPORATE THE CREATE METHOD INTO YOUR LIFE

1. Commit to daily practice: Understand that transformation isn't a one-time event. Dedicate consistent time each day—even just a few minutes—to engage with your wardrobe intentionally. Consistency is step one.

2. Become an archaeologist of your own closet: At least quarterly, pull out *everything* and reassess each piece with ruthless honesty. Ask yourself: "What story can I tell with this garment?" and "Does this spark joy or energy?" Also ask: "How does this piece make me feel? What *feeling(s)* do I associate with it?" I suggest a monthly twenty- to thirty-minute assessment and catalogue. I donate pieces regularly via this cleanout method. You do *not* want stagnant pieces creating buildup in your energy flow.

3. Prioritize energetic alignment: Before you even consider fit or trend, ask how a garment makes you *feel*. Choose pieces that elevate your energy and align with your desired emotional state for the day.

4. Embrace the "as if" principle: Dress for your future reality. If you're manifesting a new role, relationship, or mindset, select clothing that embodies the energy of that desired outcome.

5. Invest in tailoring: Recognize that perfect fit is paramount, regardless of price point. Find a reliable tailor and utilize their services for even minor adjustments; it instantly elevates your entire wardrobe.

6. Trust your intuition: Your inner wisdom is your most powerful style guide. When considering a piece, pay attention to your gut

feeling. If it feels off, it probably is. It is *always* about first asking yourself with any piece, and the first glance in the mirror: "How does this make me feel?"

7. Play with contradictions: Allow your style to be multifaceted. Embrace the yin and yang by pairing seemingly opposite elements (e.g., romantic with edgy, structured with fluid) to create visual intrigue that reflects your complex nature. When in doubt with a silhouette or outfit pairing, try this "opposites attract" strategy. This works with everything from skinny leg + bold shoulder to romantic dress + chunky grounding shoe.

8. Understand fabric frequencies: Be aware of how different fabrics impact your energy. Prioritize natural fibers like linen, wool, and organic cotton, which tend to harmonize with your body's natural frequency. Once you tap into this side of your energy, you can instantly use fabrics to shift how you are feeling physically.

9. Align with your chakras / ego centers: Learn the "language" of your body's energy centers. Consciously select colors, silhouettes, and textures that activate and support the specific qualities you want to cultivate (e.g., structured for grounding, flowing for creativity).

10. Define your archetypes: Identify your core style "moods" or archetypes (e.g., Serene, Powerful, Joyful). Use these as a daily framework for intentional dressing, allowing you to fluidly step into different aspects of yourself as needed. Have a list on standby hanging in your closet or in an accessible binder as a reminder, or keep it in a notes section on your phone.

♡ MANIFESTATION MENTOR
Mariska Hargitay

"You Have to have the AUDACITY to CREATE."

— MARISKA HARGITAY

As I was writing this book, my client Mariska Hargitay invited me to join her on the set of her show *Law & Order: Special Victims Unit*, where she's played the role of detective Olivia Benson for over twenty-five years. I jumped at the chance. Though I've been on countless sets, *Law & Order: SVU* is iconic. At some point or another, just about every New Yorker turns a corner to find the show's location vans lining the street. (They use dozens of NYC locations every season.) Besides that, bingeing seasons of *Law & Order* has gotten me through breakups and other hard times—you know the ones when you just want to shut the world out and chill on the couch in front of the TV?

I was also psyched to get the chance to see Mariska inhabit her character through the clothes. She put me in her director's chair to watch as she filmed scenes and then, in between takes, we chatted about how she personally interprets the CREATE road map.

Listening, I was reminded of how much self-awareness and self-compassion factor into how we think about fashion and style and the various ways our sense of self impacts our happiness. Over many years, Mariska's journey with dressing shifted from external validation to internal wisdom, rooted in what she describes as "integration" and "healing" through working on her 2025 documentary, *My Mom Jayne*, a deeply personal film about her mother, sex symbol movie star Jayne

Mansfield, who died in a car accident when Mariska was only three years old.

I met Mariska when she was preparing for the film's premieres, the Cannes Film Festival, and any other events and opportunities that might come up. She wanted to embrace the power of fashion for these occasions to pay homage to her mom, and I'm so grateful that she enlisted me to help her do it. During the press tour we played with super feminine shapes, textures, and colors—lots of pink, sparkle, and curve-accentuating fits. We gravitated to designers such as Carolina Herrera, Stella McCartney, and Oscar de la Renta. (The Oscar ensemble had the drama of both a sparkly cape *and* gloves.)

These gorgeous designs were paired with fantastic heirloom jewelry Mariska inherited from Jayne. I marveled watching the power of intention unfolding in such a beautiful way—honoring a special moment in time where a legacy could be lovingly carried on through personal transformation. And doing it all on a very big, public stage.

Mariska embraces the full arc of living the CREATE method, and how it can change the way you move through daily life. She has become crystal clear on the woman she wants to be and the tools she needs to keep becoming that woman. She described the shift into this new state, where she gives herself permission to surrender to possibility, to enjoy fashion, and to look for alignment everywhere, as "a world becoming technicolor."

I wanted Mariska's take on how the art of intentional dressing and how living the pillars of the CREATE method have changed her life, so we unpacked it together. Below are some ways she describes her bigger, brighter reality upon embracing her own "audacity to create." When those words fell from her lips, I immediately decided I needed to put that quote on a T-shirt. We *all* need to embrace our audacity to create. It's how we transform and, even more practically, it's how we can get shit done.

Clarity

Mariska's fundamental philosophy in getting dressed has transformed from asking "How does this look? Does this look good?" to the more intentional question "How do I want to feel?" Mariska now seeks to feel "safe, protected, soft, playful, flirty, feminine." This approach includes asking herself, "Does this bring me joy? Does this make me feel good?" and recognizing that "if it doesn't quite fit then I don't want it—there's such a discernment now, a new discernment," says Mariska, calling these moments "beautiful little victories." A recent moment of that decision-making happened when selecting jewelry for a Paris event: "I tried on this necklace and I went, 'This is exactly right.' And I was so clear about it" even though she was supposed to consider a bunch of other options.

Our days don't necessarily unfold the way we plan and, as Mariska says, "Life is difficult and challenging and shit happens. There are also those little disappointments in the day. And so now what I try to focus on are sparks of light or joy or clarity."

These sparks offer us guidance when a curveball gets thrown our way. A fitting with Mariska is always very efficient because she has harnessed this clarity in a way that instinctively she knows if a garment or element will serve how she wants to feel or what she needs to project. Clarity cuts straight to the point. And that is the point of the CREATE method.

Ritual

Central to Mariska's practice is the ritual of listening to her inner wisdom and subscribing to a mindful "one thing at a time" way of operating. She has learned to pause when overwhelmed instead of just powering through: "I really listen to myself now in a new way where if I'm feeling overwhelmed, I'll just stop," she says. "I'll just stop what I'm doing and sit down." This extends to her morning dressing routine, where she trusts "that teeny voice. That inner voice is always right and it will always guide you," she says. "If you listen to it, life's just easier."

Understanding the power of the pause is one of the huge takeaways from the CREATE method. If we don't take a beat when things get chaotic, that's when we spiral. In the process of finding the rituals that best serve you, ground you, reboot and recalibrate you, I suggest making sure one focus is to take a much-needed beat. Doing that automatically causes you to become more present. And being more present allows you to enjoy and experience things in a heightened way. I'm trying to teach my kids the value of being present—not the easiest thing to explain to a four-year-old, but over time and with practice, I know it will make sense and be one of the most valuable lessons that I impart.

Learning to not let your thoughts become a runaway train that derails your life is a key to an existence that gets perpetually better. So stop. Take a pause. Get present. Breathe. Who is that woman you want to be? What does she look like? What does she want to feel like? What does she need?

Editing

Mariska's editing process involves rigorous honesty about what serves her versus what merely looks appealing. She describes having "things in my closet that I loved" but recognizes when appearance conflicts with comfort or authenticity. She had a cool pink sequined shirt that she adored, but "it was uncomfortable and caught on stuff." For those reasons alone, it had to go. There is also the energizing boost that comes with donating and passing on things you no longer need (or want), so that energetically, you are not holding on to old versions of yourself that no longer resonate. Mariska passes on pieces to loved ones, friends, or charities.

Her honed intuition makes editing with Mariska easy, efficient, and fun. Ultimately, editing your closet is where you get to decide what fashion narrative you want to share with the world. And that should be fun.

Alignment

Alignment came with Mariska's newfound appreciation for her mother's "elegant and so feminine and powerful" style after having spent years cultivating a "sort of masculinity." She now embraces both the powerful protective armor from the show, like structured blazers and other aspects developed through playing Olivia Benson, and her desire for "super feminine" choices. This awareness, Mariska says, affects her "entire being—confidence, how I act, how I talk to people." These days, her "go-to color is pink," which she considers a "divine feminine color," and she also gravitates toward "jewel tones" especially for bold red-carpet occasions.

Truth

Since Mariska lost her mom at such a young age, the details of just getting dressed for school (let alone understanding fashion) were not a priority in her house growing up. Moving beyond the experiences of her youth where she had to be pretty self-sufficient took a long time.

When we find the courage to heal, we can accept who we are. In her mid-twenties, Mariska was shocked to find out that the man who lovingly raised her—Mickey Hargitay—was not her biological father. Her real father was Nelson Sardelli, a singer her mother had a brief affair with. Says Mariska: "I've done so much work on myself. With the secret of my father . . . and having things about my mom that I didn't want to look at. Now I'm not afraid. So, I've done the work to get the infrastructure to look at the truth now. And I realize that the only way out is through. So, is it uncomfortable? Yes. Is it a bumpy ride? Yep. Do you know what you're going to find? Nope. But if you stay the course, there's so much light and joy and freedom on the other side. There's freedom. And I think that until we go through it, we don't have freedom—and that's where the gold lies."

On getting dressed in her life today, Mariska says: "I'm not fighting against anything."

Expansion

The healing she experienced making *My Mom Jayne* has allowed Mariska to rediscover fashion and facilitated "a reintroduction and integration of those exiled parts of myself," she says, referring to those more conventionally feminine parts. She describes previously feeling like fashion was "a language that I couldn't speak and now I see it and I speak it with a new and nuanced awareness." I have watched firsthand as Mariska has upleveled her style confidence.

"No rules," she says. "Just the audacity to create."

When our chat was over and Mariska had finished filming, she changed out of Olivia Benson's detective uniform—a button down, slacks, and boots, all in dark hues—into her real clothes, which included a soft pink sweatshirt with the word *MOM* emblazoned on it. She dropped me off at the subway, where I headed home for my own style transition into mom mode, feeling inspired to become more audacious than ever.

The CREATE Method and Me

What does CREATE look like for me? Join me in my dressing room for a day in the life.

Clarity

I start every day with gratitude practice. I got one of those gratitude journals as a gift and I am obsessed with it. It's so easy. You write down what you are grateful for each day and what would make the day great, and then you do an assessment of how things went at day's end.

I then take some time to sit and do a CALM (clarity, assessment, love, mantra) check-in. For me, a CALM check-in is really about offering myself a pause and some compassion to start my day. I typically do this in bed before anything, especially if I happen to wake up anxious or not particularly rested—both common realities in working mom life these days. CALM check-ins can actually come throughout my day, before I start a fitting, walk into a shoot, or meet with a potential client. It gives me an opportunity to reboot and get centered. I think, *"How do I want to feel? What is my physical reality? How can I offer love and compassion to myself? And what's my mantra?"* My intention typically goes back to the feeling of serenity and my own quest for calm and cohesion for all the moving parts in my life.

Clarity for me is about both a micro and macro assessment: How do I want to feel today *and* later? When I keep a greater road path of intention in mind with each journey, it helps guide me with how to structure my day as I look at the givens of my schedule and what I need to set aside time for. My bigger path always ties into purpose, for being a source of inspiration, beauty, kindness, compassion, and creativity—to my family, friends, and the world. Everyone's greater intention varies and clarity can re-center you on yours and tie you back into *unity* with your world, which as Laura Day reminds us is essential. We're all in this together! Find an element of yourself that is of service, even if that is as simple as offering a lens of love to another each day, through kind words, generosity, or even inspirational example. Keep thinking of the small ways even acts of being compassionate to yourself can have ripple effects on the world around you. I keep finding that when I take the time to dress intentionally, and offer myself compassion to start my day, this act of kindness is mirrored to me throughout the day, in an exchange at the coffee shop, on the subway, with a driver, with my work team, with my family. (Kids are particularly responsive to energy and the example of how their caretakers view, treat, and love themselves.) I try to be and embody the change I want to see in the world every day. It keeps me clear and calm. Give it a try!

Ritual

Most days for me start with my intentional practice, and then in the midst of getting kids ready and sorted, I light a candle and some palo santo and sage (for real: I swirl it around the bathroom and the kitchen; I swear it does a reboot and the kids enter the room calmer) and do my vitamins, hot water with lemon (it gets my taste and digestion system activated and alkalized), and coffee (obviously). I also love adding the alkalizing powder from Sarah Wragge Wellness or AG1 greens powder to additionally alkalize pre-coffee, and I am loving ARMRA® colostrum, which further supports my gut. Since my intuition relies so heavily on my gut, and I feel triggers and stresses so immediately there, I have been trying to boost and help that region as much as possible.

I always incorporate movement into my daily routine. It might happen some days *after* I get dressed and get the kids to school—that's just what works better for our family right now—but the dream is to get it done before. I do yoga, Pilates, dance workouts, HIIT—I love it all. Some days can be pretty stacked, especially with travel, and I only have time for a ten- to fifteen-minute SotoMethod sculpt or cardio boost—and that's okay. I use this time to shake out stuck energy, calm my nerves and boost my morale, and reconnect me with my center. I also *love* getting a good foam roller or fascia roll or stretch mixed in to cleanse the tension and stretch it all out a bit more. Ever since Lo Roxburgh told me that fascia was linked to my soul, I gotta get in there.

I have gotten into the habit of choosing my outfits the night before since mornings with small kids are chaotic. I look at the day, assess my schedule, and tap into how I want to feel at said occasions. For me, a lot of power play pieces come into action for work as I need to tap into that empowered, confident Boss energy, but I also balance that with a lot of white in my wardrobe to calm my nervous system, activate some goddess, divine feminine *serene* goals, and less pattern play than I did in younger years when things were more chaotic. I tend to mix in jewelry pieces with energy from my mom and grandma (gold medallions, stacked gold rings, charm bracelets) and I always try to mix in something new, surprising, or more fashion-forward for an extra energy boost, like a chunky Roxanne Assoulin heart necklace, Eliou turquoise beads, pearls, fun costume earrings like the Schiaparelli Eyes, or mismatched stacked earrings from Jen Fisher and Jen Meyer. My James Banks code locket is a new fave pendant to rock to remind me to keep an open heart *and* maintain my energetic boundaries.

I should add that I have become equally intentional about what I wear to work out (always a matching set), nightwear (silk pjs or short sets or a beautiful nightgown—you will never ever find me sleeping in a T-shirt), and what I change into when I get home at the end of the day (think a housedress, pinstripe set, matching cashmere or cozy sweats). I always change when I get home to remove the energy of where I have been. I typically take off my jewelry, too, to further acknowledge I am crossing a threshold. These physical acts are a reminder to my senses that I am at a transition point, starting a new chapter in my day.

Editing

Ah, the edit!!!! This chapter and step are huge, for me and for you. Editing is not a one-time event but a continual process you will need to keep engaging, confronting, and negotiating what you allow into your most precious space—your closet! This sacred space houses your personalities and possibilities, and, more importantly, it is a portal to access yourself, even the *best* versions of yourself, every day.

What are my routines in this department?

BIG-PICTURE EDIT

Twice a year, I do a complete closet edit. I look at every piece and associate a feeling with it. If a piece evokes a feeling that is out of alignment with what I want in my closet arsenal, it goes. Where this gets really fun is when you catalogue it. As you invest in new pieces, you will continue to catalogue the feelings you associate with each piece. Pick three words for each piece. For example, this white blouse makes me feel elegant, effortless, and at ease. You can also associate it with an archetype—perhaps, this blouse can work with Serene and Boss vibes.

In terms of practicality, I organize my closet by categories and have all velvet hangers. This part might be a luxury, but I do recommend making sure all clothes face to the left, or at least the same direction. Keep jackets together, tops together, pants, dresses, etc. and merchandise by color, just like a store would. I like to hang sets and suits together. I think it's more practical.

Take the time to make at least five outfits for your go-to archetypes, and five outfits that really embody that feeling. Take photos of the outfits and save this library on your phone. You can even create a saved album for each archetype and each vibe to make it so much easier every day to channel how you want to feel.

EVERYDAY EDIT

What about a couple essentials, for every day? Once you have cataloged all your clothes, getting dressed becomes *so* much easier. You simply think about how you want to feel and then you can put together outfits that recognize this. Look at your listed arsenal. Is there something that immediately resonates? Go for it.

Feeling risky? Go to your risk rack and try on something that feels like a step in a new direction. Pair it with one of your go-to looks to mix it up, or a piece that matches the vibe you want to feel. For example, if it's a more architectural piece, try it with something more tailored if you are going for joyful Boss energy. Add a chunky shoe to uplevel, and make it a sneaker or boot if you need more grounding.

Alignment

Now, I wasn't joking in Chapter 6 on Alignment when I acknowledged that it is next-level stuff.

I believe learning to understand our intuition and how to use our bodies, and to better listen to them, and to better harness our energy and *innerstanding* are essential to growth and to operating in integrity every single day. Take the time to learn how fabrics feel to you, how silhouettes feel, how different proportion plays work for you. If you keep at it, your intuition to what resonates with you won't even need to be something you have to think about anymore. You will just know.

Some people are *fashion* people. They live to mix it up every single day. I like to now and then, but I think our lives flow in phases, and in the interim if you are aware of what works for you and what makes you feel great—your "style"—that can work as a go-to way to shift your energy and operate at a higher frequency every day. For now, given all the hectic schedules and moving parts, a more streamlined style approach works better for me.

It makes me feel more aligned to activate goddess energy with white clothes. It makes me feel protected when I wear black because a lot of time a lot of opinions and variables are tossed my way and I don't need to take it *all* in. I am leaning into proportions that in work life offer me empowerment, structure, ease, and effortlessness, invoking my Third Eye and Crown Chakras (see Laura Day's breakdown of how to use your body's energy centers in Chapter 6), and I shift these a bit in my roles as mother, partner, wife, and friend, all the while keeping in mind unity and cohesion amid these moving roles and moving parts. I am not dressing just for myself; I am dressing for my many roles, my purpose in this world, and the legacy I want to leave behind. Every day.

Keep at it with the alignment research. Try to learn a bit more about alignment and your body every single day—with one piece of clothing at a time. Once you find an energy with each piece, your relationship to your clothes will keep shifting, evolving, and transforming.

Truth

Ever since I became a mother I started thinking more about legacy. How do all the moving parts in my life work in cohesion with each other? How do they reflect each other and aid each other? And with regard to fashion, how do the clothing choices I make every day create a positive ripple effect to all the areas of my life? How does thinking about "the woman I want to be" help me to embody that woman, be that woman, and better serve others?

Ever since I started thinking about fashion intentionally and dressing the part of the person I want to be, everything has changed. I see myself and am seen differently, and I operate differently; things have a better flow, a better synthesis, a purpose. My moving parts are united—even amid a consistent chaos! I am not perfect, and neither is the process, but by being disciplined in my routines and systems, I allow myself the freedom and space to operate every day so that my choices are in alignment with how I want to feel and who I want to be.

To put it simply, I dress the part. I dress the change I want to see in me and the world. And it works.

Expansion

What's possible? Everything. So be discerning, be decisive, be clear, and be compassionate with yourself in the process. I am totally down for risks, loving the risk rack, and trying new things. There are countless new AI apps that make it easier than ever to try new things. When you show up for yourself you can better show up for others. Make the commitment to yourself to keep listening and to keep making choices in alignment with that ever-moving finish line.

Chapter Summary

Threading It All Together

The CREATE method didn't emerge overnight—it was born from thousands of hours of work, study, research, application, and public trials and errors. It came from excavating and translating instinctive practice into teachable, replicable steps.

That's the power of having a clear method: It transforms intuitive knowledge into something you can consciously apply. At this point in the journey, you understand that dressing with intention—using the CREATE method—is about aligning your style with the truth of who you want to be in this world so you can summon your highest self and make good things happen.

Quick Alterations to Make

View your clothing as an energy tool. Select pieces that elevate your emotional state and embody the life you're creating.

- *✗* Make a daily commitment to intentional dressing, even if brief
- *✗* Do quarterly closet audits (plus monthly twenty- to thirty-minute reviews) to remove stagnant energy and reassess each piece's emotional resonance
- *✗* Prioritize tailoring for perfect fit at any price point
- *✗* Always ask "How does this make me feel?" before considering trends
- *✗* Dress as if you're already living your desired reality
- *✗* Trust your intuition as your primary style guide
- *✗* Play with contradictions (romantic + edgy, structured + fluid) to reflect your complexity
- *✗* Align with chakras / energy centers through intentional color, silhouette, and texture choices
- *✗* Define three to five style archetypes (Serene, Powerful, Joyful, etc.) and keep them accessible for daily reference

Continue Designing Your Future

You're cultivating so much self-awareness by paying attention to how clothing choices affect your energy, mood, and confidence throughout the day. This ongoing feedback loop will continue to refine your practice. By becoming so deeply attuned, when something feels off, you'll move on without hesitation.

Also, please give yourself grace and understand that not every day will be perfect. This is very important. You're engaging in a process that asks you to make small steps rather than overhaul everything at once—but these adjustments will change your life when you commit to them.

Everything is possible when you show up for yourself. Dressing intentionally isn't just an art—it's a daily gift to yourself.

Now Let's Get Dressed

I'm so proud of you for showing up to this book, because that means you are ready to show up for your life in your full essence. Every day is a fresh opportunity to live in your integrity and to keep telling the story that is uniquely yours. With the CREATE method, you have everything you need to manifest a life in style. So it's your turn to go supernova, and I can't wait to see you shine. You don't finish this book and then you are done. You finish this book and you begin. Welcome to the journey.

I hope you'll join me at erinwalsh.com to continue on this journey with the CREATE method together! I can't wait to get intentional with you *every single day*.

Acknowledgments

THINKING BACK TO 2019, DEEP in the constancy of doing: working, mothering, and the quest for true purpose—I remember telling a friend that I wanted to write a book. I didn't know exactly what would be in it or how it would unfold, but I knew there was a problem I wanted to solve. I was frustrated and saddened by how the fashion industry as a whole, and even just the simple daily act of getting dressed, seemed to make every woman I knew feel inadequate—from my famous clients to my aunts in the Midwest. The desire to alleviate that style-driven suffering was the genesis of this book. So here it is. I hope you find solace—and solutions—in these pages.

This journey would not have been possible had I not decided to think magically, which led me to miracle worker Gabby Bernstein, a talented spiritual teacher and, to me, wunderkind healer. She introduced me to the inimitable Michele Promaulayko, who worked with me in creating this book in a way that honored the mission with humility, candor, wit, intelligence, and a fierce allegiance to guiding my voice to allow for elegance and accessibility. Michele, thank you for being my partner.

To my fashion soulmate, Anne Hathaway, who wrote the foreword to this book, and who has upleveled my soul and my style through our wildly joyful collaborations in life and fashion. I love you, girl. GWFG.

To all the women who have inspired me in my twenty-plus (and counting) years in the fashion industry—including the ones who pushed me, like my first boss at *Vogue*, Phyllis Posnick. Also, Samira Nasr, who believed in me before I knew how to believe in myself, and Elizabeth Saltzman, my fashion fairy god-sister, who helped me get to the next level in my career.

To my friend and confidant Nicole Caruso, a publicist who offered me huge opportunities with her biggest clients *before* we were friends, launching my celebrity styling career. You have always seen my passion and my potential.

To the muses who embody the deeply personal, vulnerable, and crucial work of speaking your soul through what you wear: Sarah Jessica Parker, Kerry Washington, Kristen Wiig, Anne Hathaway, Selena Gomez, Thandiwe Newton, Maggie Gyllenhaal, Greta Gerwig, Ashley Park, Mariska Hargitay, Mindy Kaling, Ariana DeBose, Beanie Feldstein, Elizabeth Banks, Juno Temple, Alison Brie, Nazanin Boniadi, Lucy Hale, Dove Cameron, Ruth Wilson, Adriana Lima, Lily Aldridge, Adrienne Warren, Cleo Wade, Cobie Smulders, and many more—thank you for being game to collaborate, expand, experiment, and commit to the idea that what we wear can be so very powerful when we get intentional about it.

To Aleen Keshishian, who has encouraged me to get more intentional than ever—I am so grateful for your wisdom and guidance.

To my fashionable friends Jennifer Fisher, Gucci Westman Neville, Fabiola Beracasa Beckman, Meredith Melling, and my celebrity stylist peers—thank you for always showing me new ways to dream with clothes.

To the wonderful women (and the few exceptional men!) I interviewed for this book—Diane von Fürstenberg, Jennifer Fisher, Sara Blakely, Zanna Roberts Rassi, Hilary Hoffman, Laura Day, Kerry Washington, Mariska Hargitay, Mindy Kaling, Gabby Bernstein, Jenn Hyman, Marie Forleo, Elise Loehnen, Lauren Roxburgh, Michelle K. Gagnon, Dr. Tara Swart, Aurora James, Amanda Gibby Peters, Oliver Walsh, Rachel Zoe, Michael Kors, Zac Posen, and more—your words and wisdom brought color, insight, and practical magic to my method.

To my brilliant Danish friends at NR2154, Julie Lysbo and Jacob Wildschiødtz, thank you for your design talent—you make every creative project more imaginative.

To the entire team at HarperOne—thank you for saying yes! Especially my editor, Stephanie Smith, who took a chance on me and was an absolute dream to work with. Thank you for seeing and understanding my vision.

To my rock star agent team at A-Frame Agency, Alex Feldman, Noelle Keshishian, Lauren Moberg, and more—thank you for always supporting my quest to keep expanding. To Julia Bodner and Envisionary Management—thank you for helping me imagine this next chapter.

To Tia Ikemoto and Kari Stuart at Creative Artists Agency (CAA). Thank you for so competently and calmly shepherding the process of bringing this book to the world. You always made sure I was in the best hands.

To the Lede Company, thank you for helping to amplify the movement born from this book. I can't wait to see how far we reach.

To Carissa Schumacher, thank you for your indispensable insight and support.

To Valerie Mya, thank you for asking me the life-changing question: How do you want to feel? That query is both my mantra and my North Star.

To Kait Walsh, who worked tirelessly to perfect the gorgeous, magnetic, and very me illustrations that accompany this tome.

To my mom, Jane, and her mom, Jane—thank you for reminding me that when we get intentional about what we wear, everything (and anything) is within reach.

To my loving husband, Christian Högstedt, my valiant partner in life. It can't be easy being married to someone who always wants more, but you never question my insatiable desire to grow, expand, do, seek, and manifest. Thank you for seeing and supporting me and our wild and beautiful kids, Matilda, Jude, and Hugo. You are my calm and my comfort. I love you.

Notes

Introduction

1. The Royal Swedish Academy of Sciences, "The Nobel Prize in Physics 2022," NobelPrize.org, Nobel Prize Outreach AB, October 4, 2022, https://www.nobelprize.org/prizes/physics/2022/press-release/.
2. "Einstein's 'Spooky Action at a Distance' Paradox Older Than Thought," *MIT Technology Review*, March 7, 2012.
3. Hajo Adam and Adam D. Galinsky, "Enclothed Cognition," *Journal of Experimental Social Psychology* 48, no. 4 (2012): 918–25.
4. Kelly Wearstler, "WARDROBE MEETS WORKFLOW: My Style at the Studio," *Wearstler World*, July 22, 2025, https://wearstlerworld.substack.com/p/wardrobe-meets-workflow-my-style.

Chapter 1: Why You Don't Know What the Eff to Wear

1. Joe Dispenza, *Breaking the Habit of Being Yourself: How to Lose Your Mind and Create a New One* (Carlsbad, CA: Hay House, 2012), 18–19.
2. Eric I. Knudsen, "Sensitive Periods in the Development of the Brain and Behavior," *Journal of Cognitive Neuroscience* 16, no. 8 (2004): 1412–25.
3. Center on the Developing Child, Harvard University, "InBrief: The Science of Early Childhood Development," 2007, accessed August 20, 2025, https://developingchild.harvard.edu/resources/inbriefs/inbrief-science-of-ecd/.
4. Jon Kabat-Zinn, *Wherever You Go, There You Are: Mindfulness Meditation in Everyday Life* (New York: Hyperion, 1994), 4–7.
5. Albert Ellis, *Reason and Emotion in Psychotherapy* (New York: Lyle Stuart, 1962), 36–42; and Albert Ellis and Debbie Joffe Ellis, *Rational Emotive Behavior Therapy* (Washington, DC: American Psychological Association, 2011), 15–28.
6. Timothy D. Wilson, "The Adaptive Unconscious," *American Psychologist* 57, no. 11 (2002): 817–34.
7. Fabienne Picard, "Ecstatic or Mystical Experience Through Epilepsy," *Journal of Cognitive Neuroscience* 35, no. 9 (2023): 1372–81, https://pmc.ncbi.nlm.nih.gov/articles/PMC10513764/.

Chapter 2: Practical Magic

1. Linda Smolak, "Body Image Development in Children," in *Body Image: A Handbook of Science, Practice, and Prevention*, eds. Thomas F. Cash and Linda Smolak (New York: Guilford Press, 2011), 67–76.
2. J. Kevin Thompson and Eric Stice, "Thin-Ideal Internalization: Mounting Evidence for a New Risk Factor for Body-Image Disturbance and Eating Pathology," *Current Directions in Psychological Science* 10, no. 5 (2001): 181–83.
3. "The Hollywood Reporter's 2023 List of the Most Powerful Celebrity Stylists," *The Hollywood Reporter*, April 9, 2023, https://www.hollywoodreporter.com/feature/best-celebrity-stylists-2023-1235360354/.

Chapter 3: Clarity

1. Gabby Bernstein, host, "4 Ways to Change Your Mood Fast," *Dear Gabby* podcast, August 21, 2025, accessed August 21, 2025, https://gabbybernstein.com/podcast/4-ways-to-change-your-mood-fast/.

Chapter 4: Ritual

1. Jacquelyn Cafasso, "Binaural Beats: Sleep, Therapy, and Meditation," Healthline, August 28, 2024, https://www.healthline.com/health/binaural-beats.

Chapter 5: Editing

1. Mark Holgate, "Steven Klein and Phyllis Posnick Share the Stories Behind Some of Their Greatest Vogue Images," *Vogue*, November 22, 2022, https://www.vogue.com/article/steven-klein-book.
2. Marie Kondo, "Reflections on Motherhood," KonMari, accessed December 11, 2025, https://konmari.com/marie-kondo-thoughts-on-motherhood/.
3. Marie Kondo, *The Life-Changing Magic of Tidying Up: The Japanese Art of Decluttering and Organizing* (New York: Ten Speed Press, 2014).

Chapter 7: Truth

1. Mel Robbins, host, "If You Only Listen to One Podcast Today, Make It This One," produced by Emma Grede, *The Mel Robbins Podcast*, August 2025, 1:32:00, https://open.spotify.com/episode/4t6FgpzRDAqwvC02Z2kNLq.
2. Daisy Murray, "Emma Grede Is the Celebrity Fashion Brand Mogul with the Midas Touch," *Elle UK*, August 8, 2023, https://www.elle.com/uk/fashion/a36740484/emma-grede-interview/.
3. Ibid.
4. Mel Robbins, "If You Only Listen."
5. Ibid.
6. Ibid.
7. Ibid.
8. Ibid.
9. Ibid.
10. Damien Fry and Simon Robins, "The Working Wardrobe with Emma Grede," PORTER, accessed September 2, 2025, https://www.net-a-porter.com/en-us/porter/article-2b6bdb885ee8f3ca/fashion/art-of-style/emma-grede.
11. Ibid.
12. Elizabeth Grace Coyne, "Glitz, Glamour and the Resurgence of 'Old Hollywood' on the Red Carpet," *Forbes*, March 5, 2025, https://www.forbes.com/sites/elizabethgracecoyne/2025/03/06/glitz-glamour--the-resurgence-of-old-hollywood-on-the-red-carpet/.
13. "Superstylist Erin Walsh Can Turn a Star's Style Around," *The Financial Times*, December 25, 2023, accessed August 31, 2025, https://www.ft.com/content/1aabc90f-5e04-439a-93b2-e78834576be2.
14. Leigh Nordstrom, "Anne Hathaway Enters Her 'Queen Era,' Reprising Iconic Roles and Cementing Her Reign in Fashion," *Women's Wear Daily*, December 2024, accessed August 31, 2025, https://wwd.com/eye/people/anne-hathaway-the-devil-wears-prada-1236736768/.
15. Jo-Ann Furniss, "Miuccia Prada on Being Shy, Working with Her Husband and Her Mad Office with a Helter Skelter," *The Telegraph*, accessed August 31, 2025, https://www.telegraph.co.uk/fashion/people/miuccia-prada-on-being-shy-working-with-her-husband-and-her-mad/.

Chapter 8: Expansion

1. Brené Brown, *Daring Greatly: How the Courage to Be Vulnerable Transforms the Way We Live, Love, Parent, and Lead* (New York: Avery, 2012).